Apache Superset Quick Start Guide

Develop interactive visualizations by creating user-friendly dashboards

Shashank Shekhar

BIRMINGHAM - MUMBAI

Apache Superset Quick Start Guide

Commissioning Editor: Sunith Shetty
Acquisition Editor: Siddharth Mandal
Content Development Editor: Kirk Dsouza
Technical Editor: Suwarna Patil
Copy Editor: Safis Editing
Project Coordinator: Hardik Bhinde
Proofreader: Safis Editing
Indexer: Tejal Daruwale Soni
Graphics: Alishon Mendonsa
Production Coordinator: Tom Scaria

First published: December 2018

Production reference: 1141218

Published by Packt Publishing Ltd.
Livery Place
35 Livery Street
Birmingham
B3 2PB, UK.

ISBN 978-1-78899-224-4

www.packtpub.com

`mapt.io`

Mapt is an online digital library that gives you full access to over 5,000 books and videos, as well as industry leading tools to help you plan your personal development and advance your career. For more information, please visit our website.

Why subscribe?

- Spend less time learning and more time coding with practical eBooks and Videos from over 4,000 industry professionals

- Improve your learning with Skill Plans built especially for you

- Get a free eBook or video every month

- Mapt is fully searchable

- Copy and paste, print, and bookmark content

Packt.com

Did you know that Packt offers eBook versions of every book published, with PDF and ePub files available? You can upgrade to the eBook version at `www.packt.com` and as a print book customer, you are entitled to a discount on the eBook copy. Get in touch with us at `customercare@packtpub.com` for more details.

At `www.packt.com`, you can also read a collection of free technical articles, sign up for a range of free newsletters, and receive exclusive discounts and offers on Packt books and eBooks.

Foreword

I've always thought good problem-solving has a certain sound—like that of a key turning in a lock, with a firm but smooth turn. And then there's this click and a soft ting. You can hear it, right? It has just the right balance of standing out but not making a fuss. You can hear it, but it's also understated.

As much as we would love to hear this sound more often, the locks that we encounter every day are not that simple. Executing a project successfully is not as common a phenomenon as it sounds. Doing business is tough. It always has been. And the more complex the operations, the tougher it gets. And it is tough because, sometimes, we make it so by connecting the dots in slightly different ways.

Dashboards give you a sense of the situation, or a scan of how everything went down, giving us a feedback loop to what happened and what resulted—which can help us make better decisions, every day, with visualized data on demand.

Whether you are a business owner, contributing to a business, or just someone trying to make a system work in your everyday life, having a dashboard is almost an intuitive, mental need of seeing a bunch of dots in front of us, and being able to connect them.

And so, being able to pull data easily and arrange it nicely on a table for everyone to see is an ability that has the power to change the entire process of doing work. Increasingly, we have been seeing how, similar to coding, interest in this particular skill has touched programmers, managers, designers, marketers, CXOs, and even just individuals buying groceries.

To me, the essence of this book lies in its attempt to democratize a skill that empowers people in a way that has never happened before, using technologies that anyone can access and build on. The reliability and power to create dashboards allows anyone to uncover insights, seek truth, and use intelligence to make better decisions. So, if you are someone who has been sitting on the sidelines, this book could be the perfect wingman to enter the playground with, and change the game.

Sumit Saurav

Contributors

About the author

Shashank Shekhar is a data analyst and open source enthusiast. He has contributed to Superset and pymc3 (the Python Bayesian machine learning library), and maintains several public repositories on machine learning and data analysis projects of his own on GitHub. He heads up the data science team at HyperTrack, where he designs and implements machine learning algorithms to obtain insights from movement data. Previously, he worked at Amino on claims data. He has worked as a data scientist in Silicon Valley for 5 years. His background is in systems engineering and optimization theory, and he carries that perspective when thinking about data science, biology, culture, and history.

I would like to take this opportunity to thank my mentors, Ashish Anand, Prashant Ishwar, Prashant Kukde, and Sameera Podduri, for guiding me and setting me up on a path where I could learn about my interests and improve the skills that I required while doing so. I was lucky enough to meet them over the course of the last six years. I owe my success in writing this book, and the many goals that I am motivated to achieve in the future, to them.

About the reviewer

Stephan Adams is a software engineer working in adtech in New York City. An electrical engineer by training, he graduated with an MS from UC Berkeley in 2013. He currently works on building systems for serving massive datasets in real time to heavy traffic loads. In his spare time, Stephan enjoys playing volleyball.

Packt is searching for authors like you

If you're interested in becoming an author for Packt, please visit `authors.packtpub.com` and apply today. We have worked with thousands of developers and tech professionals, just like you, to help them share their insight with the global tech community. You can make a general application, apply for a specific hot topic that we are recruiting an author for, or submit your own idea.

Table of Contents

Preface

Apache Superset is a modern, open source, enterprise-ready **Business Intelligence** (**BI**) web application. Connecting it to a SQL database allows you to create real-time data visualizations and BI dashboards. This book gets you started with making the best use of Superset for your organization.

Who this book is for

This book is for data analysts, BI professionals, and developers who want to learn Apache Superset. If you want to create interactive dashboards from SQL databases, this book is what you need.

What this book covers

Chapter 1, *Getting Started with Data Exploration*, teaches you how to install Superset, add a database, create a dashboard, and share a dashboard with users. We will train ourselves to be ready to add additional databases and tables, as well as to create new visualizations and dashboards.

Chapter 2, *Configuring Superset and Using SQL Lab*, shows you how to configure a Superset web server for your runtime environment needs using the superset_config.py file. We will look at the configuration parameters that can make Superset secure and scalable to match optimal trade-offs. We will replace SQLite metadata with a PostgreSQL database and configure a web app to use it as the database.

Chapter 3, *User Authentication and Permissions*, looks at how to allow new users to register on the Superset web app with their Google accounts. We will explore the security tools available to the administrator, such as activity logs and user statistics.

Chapter 4, *Visualizing Data in a Column*, helps you understand columnar data through distribution plots, point-wise comparison with a reference columns, and charts.

Chapter 5, *Comparing Feature Values*, involves two datasets that you will use to compare prices of food commodities. We will make use of five chart types that will help in giving us a better understanding of how we can correlate between the two sets of data.

Chapter 6, *Drawing Connections between Entity Columns*, looks at visualizing relationships as graphs instead of coordinates on
orthogonal axes. We will learn about the approaches for visualizing and analyzing dataset with entities and a value quantifying some type of relationship.

Chapter 7, *Mapping Data That Has Location Information*, continues the trend of analyzing geographical regions by working with location data. We will visualize location data as scatter plots on maps and then we will plot arcs and lines on a map.

Chapter 8, *Building Dashboards*, is where we will make some beautiful dashboards and complete our Superset quick start journey. We will try to organize the charts such that the dashboard is effective at coherently communicating those answers.

To get the most out of this book

This book will make a great choice for collaborative data analysis work within a cross-functional team of data analysts, business professionals, and software engineers.

Many common analytical questions on data can be addressed using the charts, which are easy to use.

A working knowledge of Python will be an advantage but is not necessary to understand this book.

Download the example code files

You can download the example code files for this book from your account at www.packt.com. If you purchased this book elsewhere, you can visit www.packt.com/support and register to have the files emailed directly to you.

You can download the code files by following these steps:

1. Log in or register at www.packt.com.
2. Select the **SUPPORT** tab.
3. Click on **Code Downloads & Errata**.
4. Enter the name of the book in the **Search** box and follow the onscreen instructions.

Once the file is downloaded, please make sure that you unzip or extract the folder using the latest version of:

- WinRAR/7-Zip for Windows
- Zipeg/iZip/UnRarX for Mac
- 7-Zip/PeaZip for Linux

The code bundle for the book is also hosted on GitHub at https://github.com/PacktPublishing/Superset-Quick-Start-Guide. In case there's an update to the code, it will be updated on the existing GitHub repository.

We also have other code bundles from our rich catalog of books and videos available at https://github.com/PacktPublishing/. Check them out!

Download the color images

We also provide a PDF file that has color images of the screenshots/diagrams used in this book. You can download it here: https://www.packtpub.com/sites/default/files/downloads/9781788992244_Color Images.pdf.

Conventions used

There are a number of text conventions used throughout this book.

CodeInText: Indicates code words in text, database table names, folder names, filenames, file extensions, pathnames, dummy URLs, user input, and Twitter handles. Here is an example: "Our datasets will be public tables from Google BigQuery and .csv files from a variety of web resources, which we will upload to PostgreSQL."

A block of code is set as follows:

```
export SUPERSET_UPDATE_PERMS=0
gunicorn -w 3
 -k gevent
 --timeout 120
 -b 0.0.0.0:8088
 superset:app
```

Any command-line input or output is written as follows:

```
sudo apt-get install build-essential libssl-dev libffi-dev python-dev
python-pip libsasl2-dev libldap2-dev
```

Bold: Indicates a new term, an important word, or words that you see onscreen. For example, words in menus or dialog boxes appear in the text like this. Here is an example: "After launching, on the **VM instances** screen, we can see that our g1-small GCE instance is up and running!"

Warnings or important notes appear like this.

Tips and tricks appear like this.

Get in touch

Feedback from our readers is always welcome.

General feedback: If you have questions about any aspect of this book, mention the book title in the subject of your message and email us at customercare@packtpub.com.

Errata: Although we have taken every care to ensure the accuracy of our content, mistakes do happen. If you have found a mistake in this book, we would be grateful if you would report this to us. Please visit www.packt.com/submit-errata, selecting your book, clicking on the Errata Submission Form link, and entering the details.

Piracy: If you come across any illegal copies of our works in any form on the Internet, we would be grateful if you would provide us with the location address or website name. Please contact us at copyright@packt.com with a link to the material.

If you are interested in becoming an author: If there is a topic that you have expertise in and you are interested in either writing or contributing to a book, please visit authors.packtpub.com.

Reviews

Please leave a review. Once you have read and used this book, why not leave a review on the site that you purchased it from? Potential readers can then see and use your unbiased opinion to make purchase decisions, we at Packt can understand what you think about our products, and our authors can see your feedback on their book. Thank you!

For more information about Packt, please visit `packt.com`.

1
Getting Started with Data Exploration

Apache Superset is a web platform for creating data visualizations and telling stories with data using dashboards. Packing visualizations in a dashboard is fun, and dashboards render updates to the visualizations in real time.

The best part is that Superset has a very interactive user experience. Programming knowledge is not required for using Superset.

Superset makes it easy to share and collaborate on data analytics work. It has user roles and permission management built into it as core components. This makes it a great choice for data analysis work collaboration between a cross functional team of data analysts, business professionals, and software engineers.

There all sorts of charts to make on Superset. Many common analytical questions on data can be addressed using the charts, which are easy to use. In this book, we will do data exploration and analysis of different types of datasets. In the process, we will try to understand different aspects of Superset.

In this chapter, we will learn about the following:

- Datasets
- Installing Superset
- Sharing Superset
- Configuring Superset
- Adding a database
- Adding a table

- Creating a chart
- Uploading a CSV file
- Configuring a table schema
- Customizing the visualization
- Making a dashboard

Datasets

We will be working on a variety of datasets in this book, and we will analyze their data. We will make many charts along the way. Here is how we will go about it:

- Visualizing data distributions:
    - Headlines
    - Distributions
    - Comparisons

- Finding trends in time series or multi-feature datasets:
    - Joint distributions with time series data
    - Joint distributions with a size feature
    - Joint distributions
- Discovering hierarchical and graphical relationships between features:
    - Hierarchical maps
    - Path maps
- Plotting features with location information on maps:
    - Heatmaps using Mapbox
    - 2D maps using Mapbox
    - 3D maps using MapGL
    - World map

Superset plugs into any SQL database that has a Python SQLAlchemy connector, such as PostgreSQL, MySQL, SQLite, MongoDB, and Snowflake. The data stored in any of the databases is fetched for making charts. Most database documents have a requirement for the Python SQLAlchemy connector.

In this book, we will use **Google BigQuery** and **PostgreSQL** as our database. Our datasets will be public tables from Google BigQuery and `.csv` files from a variety of web resources, which we will upload to PostgreSQL. The datasets cover topics such as Ethereum, globally traded commodities, airports, flight routes, and a reading list of books, because the generating process for each of these datasets is different. It will be interesting to visualize and analyze the datasets.

Hopefully, the experience that we will gain over the course of this book will help us in becoming effective at using Superset for data visualization and dashboarding.

Installing Superset

Let's get started by making a Superset web app server. We will cover security, user roles, and permissions for the web app in the next chapter.

Instead of a local machine, one can also choose to set up Superset in the cloud. This way, we can even share our Superset web app with authenticated users via an internet browser (for example, Firefox or Chrome).

We will be using **Google Compute Engine** (GCE) for the Superset server. You can use the link `https://console.cloud.google.com` and set up your account.

After you have set up your account, go to the URL `https://console.cloud.google.com/apis/credentials/serviceaccountkey` to download a file, `` `<project_id>.json` ``. Save this somewhere safe. This is the Google Cloud authorization JSON key file. We will copy the contents of this file to our GCE instance after we launch it. Superset uses the information in this file to authenticate itself to Google BigQuery.

GCE instances are very easy to configure and launch. Anyone with a Google account can use it. After logging in to you Google account, use this URL: `https://console.cloud.google.com/compute/instances`. Here, launch a g1-small (**1 vCPU, 1.7 GB** memory) instance with default settings. When we have to set up Superset for a large number of concurrent users (greater than five), we should choose higher compute power instances.

After launching, on the **VM instances** screen we can see our g1-small GCE instance is up and running:

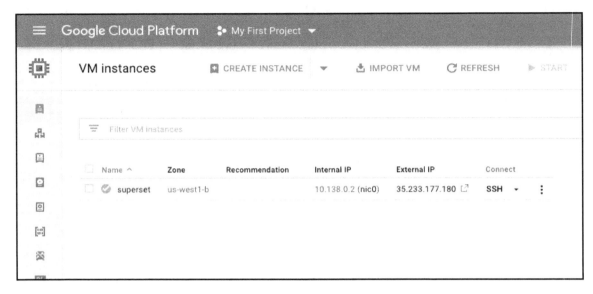

GCE dashboard on Google Cloud Platform

Sharing Superset

We will need to share our Superset web app with others, and for that we will have to figure out the URL users can use to access it through their internet browsers.

The standard format of a web server URL is `http://{address}:{port number}`.

The default port for Superset is `8088`. On a locally run Superset web app server, the address is `localhost`. Servers on internal networks are available on their internal IP address. Web apps on cloud services such as GCE or **Amazon Elastic Compute** have the machine's external IP as the address.

On GCE's **VM instances** screen, an external IP is displayed for each instance that is started. A new external IP is generated for every new instance. In the following screenshot, the external IP specified is 35.233.177.180. To share the server with registered users on the internet, we make a note of the external IP on our own screens:

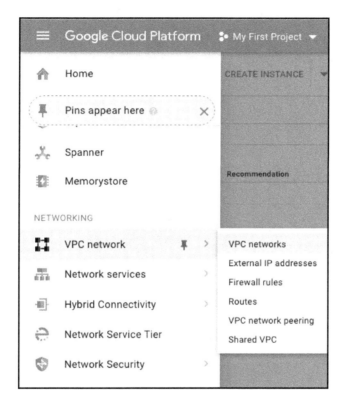

The sidebar on Google Cloud Platform

To allow users to access the port, we need to go to **VPC network** | **Firewall rules** and **Create a firewall rule** that will open port 8088 for users. We can use the field values shown in the following screenshot for the rule:

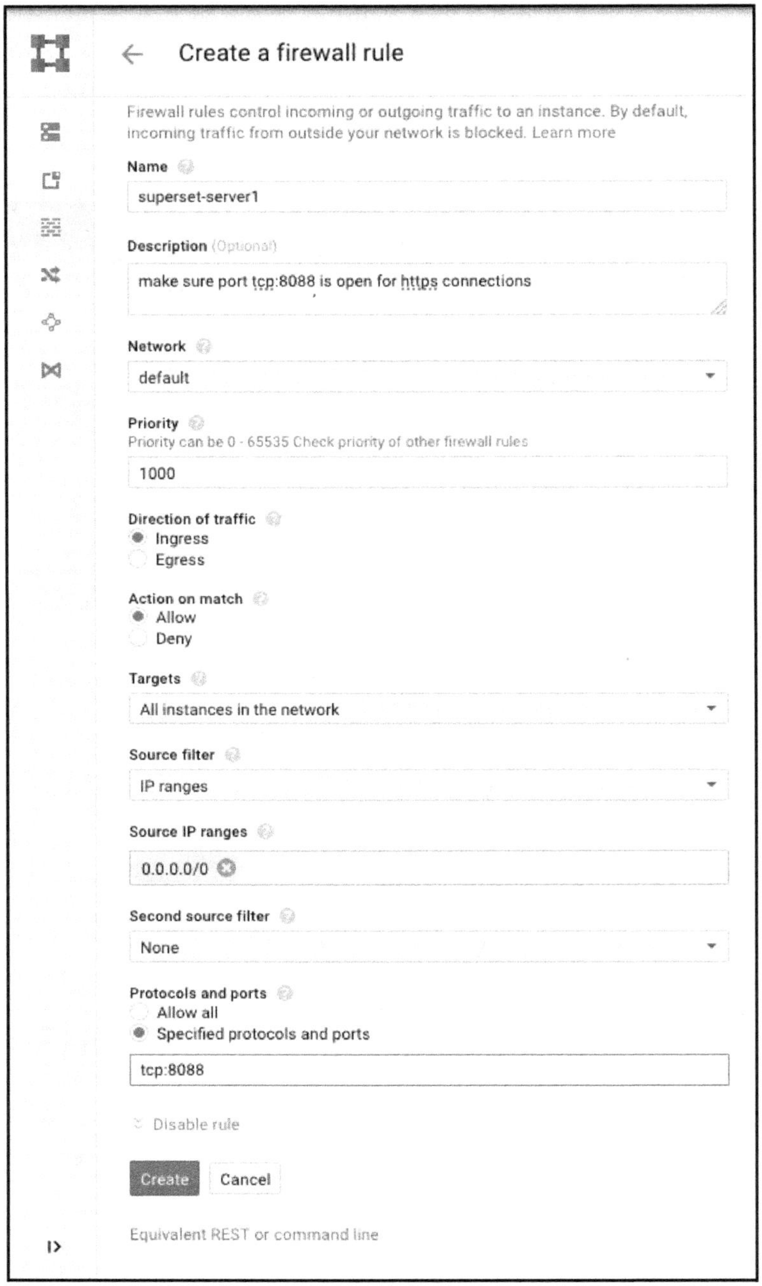

Firewall rule setup

Now, we are ready to install Superset!

Before we proceed, use the ssh option to open a Terminal that is connected to the GCE instance while staying inside your browser. This is one of the many amazing features of GCE.

In the Terminal, we will run some commands to install the dependencies and configure Superset for our first dashboard:

```
# 1) Install os-level dependencies
sudo apt-get install build-essential libssl-dev libffi-dev python-dev
python-pip libsasl2-dev libldap2-dev
# 2) Check for Python 2.7
python --version
# 3) Install pip
wget https://bootstrap.pypa.io/get-pip.py
sudo python get-pip.py
# 4) Install virtualenv
sudo pip install --upgrade virtualenv
# 5) Install virtualenvironment manager
sudo pip install virtualenvwrapper
source /usr/local/bin/virtualenvwrapper.sh
echo 'source /usr/local/bin/virtualenvwrapper.sh' >> ~/.bash_profile
# 6) Make virtual environment
mkvirtualenv supervenv
# 7) Install superset and virtualenv in the new virtual environment
(supervenv) pip install superset
(supervenv) pip install virtualenv virtualenvwrapper
# 8) Install database connector
(supervenv) pip install pybigquery
# 9) Create and open an authentication file for BigQuery
(supervenv) vim ~/.google_cdp_key.json
# 10) Copy and paste the contents of <project_id>.json key file to
~/.google_cdp_key.json
# 11) Load the new authentication file
(supervenv) echo 'export
GOOGLE_APPLICATION_CREDENTIALS="$HOME/.google_cdp_key.json"' >>
~/.bash_profile
(supervenv) source ~/.bash_profile
```

Configuring Superset

Superset uses the Flask-AppBuilder framework (`fabmanager`) to store and manage data for authentication, user permissions, and user roles in Superset.

After installing `fabmanager` in the Python virtual environment, we use the `create-admin` command in `fabmanager` and specify Superset as the app. The Flask-AppBuilder framework will create a metadata database using SQLite by default in the `~/.superset` location:

```
# On the Terminal to setup FlaskAppBuilder for superset on GCE
# Create an admin user (you will be prompted to set username, first and
last name before setting a password)
(supervenv) fabmanager create-admin --app superset
```

After creating the admin user for the Superset app, we have to run the following commands to create tables and update columns in the metadata database:

```
# Initialize the database
(supervenv) superset db upgrade

# Creates default roles and permissions
(supervenv) superset init
```

We can do a sanity check to verify that the metadata database has been created in the expected location. For this, we install `sqlite3` to query the SQLite metadata database:

```
# Install sqlite3
(superenv) sudo apt-get install sqlite3
# Navigate to the home directory
(supervenv) cd ~/.superset
# Verify database is created
(supervenv) sqlite3
> .open superset.db
> .tables
sqlite> .tables
ab_permission annotation_layer logs
ab_permission_view clusters metrics
ab_permission_view_role columns query
ab_register_user css_templates saved_query
ab_role dashboard_slices slice_user
ab_user dashboard_user slices
ab_user_role dashboards sql_metrics
ab_view_menu datasources table_columns
access_request dbs tables
alembic_version favstar url
annotation keyvalue
```

Finally, let's start the Superset web server:

```
# run superset webserver
(supervenv) superset runserver
```

Go to `http://<your_machines_external_ip>:8088` in your Chrome or Firefox web browser. The external IP I used is the one specified for the GCE instance I am using. Open the web app in your browser and log in with the `admin` credentials you entered when using the `create-admin` command on `fabmanager`.

After the login screen, you will see the welcome screen of your Superset web app:

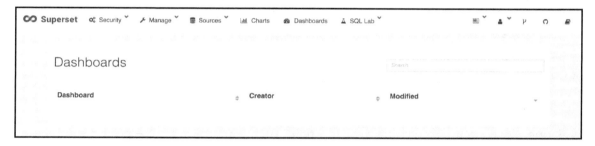

Dashboards list

Adding a database

The navigation bar lists all the features. The **Sources** section is where you will create and maintain database integrations and configure table schemas to use as sources of data.

Any SQL database that has a SQLAlchemy connector such as PostgreSQL, MySQL, SQLite, MongoDB, and Snowflake can work with Superset.

Depending on the databases that we connect to Superset, the corresponding SQLAlchemy connectors have to be installed:

Database	PyPI package
MySQL	mysqlclient
PostgreSQL	psycopg2
Presto	pyhive
Hive	pyhive
Oracle	cx_oracle
SQLite	Included in Superset

Snowflake	`snowflake-sqlalchemy`
Redshift	`sqlalchemy-redshift`
MS SQL	`pymssql`
Impala	`impyla`
Spark SQL	`pyhive`
Greenplum	`psycopg2`
Athena	`PyAthenaJDBC>1.0.9`
Vertica	`sqlalchemy-vertica-python`
ClickHouse	`sqlalchemy-clickhouse`
Kylin	`kylinpy`
BigQuery	`pybigquery`

It is recommended that you use a database that supports the creation of views. When columns from more than one table have to be fetched for visualization, views of those joins can be created in the database and visualized on Superset, because table joins are not supported in Superset.

SQL query execution for fetching data and rendering visualizations is done at the database level, and Superset only fetches results afterwards. A database with a query execution engine that scales with your data will make your dashboard more real time.

In this book, we will work with public datasets available in Google BigQuery. We have already installed a connector for BigQuery in our installation routine, using the `pip install pybigquery` command. We have set up authentication for BigQuery using a key file. You should verify that, by confirming that the environment variable points to the valid key file:

```
echo $GOOGLE_APPLICATION_CREDENTIALS
# It should return
> /home/<your user name>/.google_cdp_key.json
```

Now, let's add BigQuery as a database in three steps:

1. Select the **Databases** option from the drop-down list and create (**+**) your first database
2. Set **Database** to `superset-bigquery` and **SQLAlchemy URI** to `bigquery://`
3. Save the database

You can verify the database connection by clicking on the **Test Connection** button; it should return **Seems OK!** as follows:

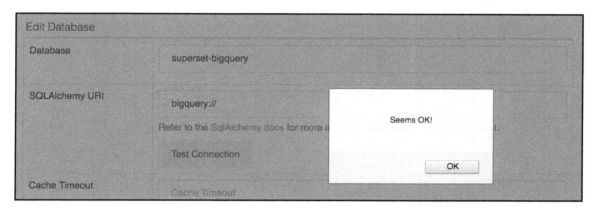

Seems OK! dialog box is generated when test connection to database is successful

Adding a table

We will add the questions table from the Stack Overflow public dataset at `https://cloud.google.com/bigquery/public-data/stackoverflow` in three steps:

1. Select the **Tables** option from the drop-down list, and create your first table
2. Set values in **Database** to `superset-bigquery` and **Table Name** to `bigquery-public-data.stackoverflow.posts_questions`

3. **Save** the table:

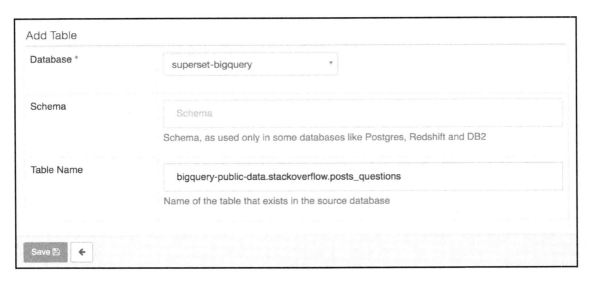

Select the database and insert the table name identifier in the form

Creating a visualization

That was smooth! You were able to add your first database and table to Superset. Now, it's time for the fun part, which is visualizing and analyzing the data. In **Table**, we will find the `bigquery-public-data.stackoverflow.posts_questions` listed as follows:

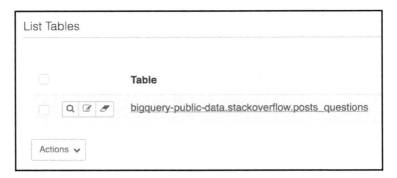

List Tables shows all available tables that can be used to make charts

When you click on it, it will take you to the chart UI:

Options available to modify the data visualized in the chart

Here, we will make a time series plot of the number of questions posted by **year**. In the **Data** tab, the **Time** section is used to restrict data by a temporal column value. We do not want to restrict data for the time series plot. We can clear the **Since** field.

In order to add axis labels to the line chart, select the **Style** tab and add descriptions in the **X Axis Label** and **Y Axis Label** fields:

Style form for the chart

Set **year** as **Time Grain** and **COUNT(*)** as the **Metrics**. Finally, hit **Run Query**:

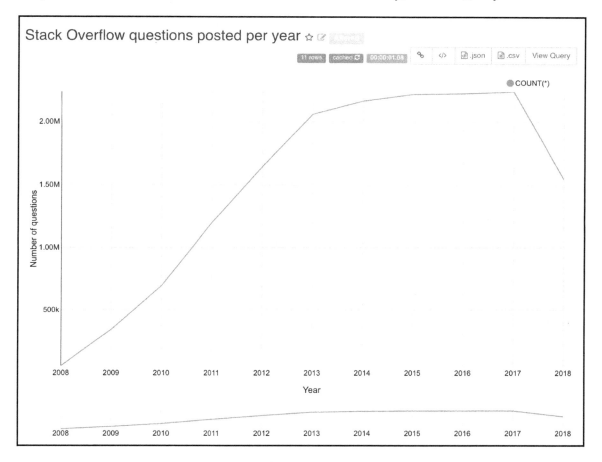

Line chart showing total number of questions posted on Stack Overflow from 2008-2018

We have our first visualization! We can see how the number of questions grew quickly from 2008-2013. Now, **Save** the visualization, so that we can add it to our dashboard later:

A name and dashboard can be assigned to the chart on the Save form

Uploading a CSV

In many types of analytical work, data is available in CSV or Excel files and not in a database. You can use the **Upload a CSV** feature to upload CSVs as tables in Superset, without parent database integration.

We will get some real data to test this. Let's download the Ethereum transaction history from `http://etherscan.io` and create a new table:

```
curl https://etherscan.io/chart/tx?output=csv > /tmp/eth_txn.csv
  % Total     % Received % Xferd  Average Speed   Time    Time     Time
Current
                                 Dload  Upload   Total   Spent    Left
Speed
100 35279    0 35279    0     0    98k      0 --:--:-- --:--:-- --:--:--
98k
```

```
# create a sqlite database to store the csv
cd ~/.superset
# this will create a sqlite database, quit after it opens the console
sqlite3 upload_csv.db
```

Edit Database

Database	upload_csv
SQLAlchemy URI	sqlite:////Users/shashankshekhar/.superset/upload_csv.db

Refer to the SqlAlchemy docs for more information on how to structure your URI.

Test Connection

Cache Timeout	Cache Timeout

Extra	{
	 "metadata_params": {},
	 "engine_params": {}
	 }

JSON string containing extra configuration elements. The `engine_params` object gets unpacked into the sqlalchemy create_engine call, while the `metadata_params` gets unpacked into the sqlalchemy.MetaData call.

Expose in SQL Lab	☑

Expose this DB in SQL Lab

Allow Run Sync	☑

Allow users to run synchronous queries, this is the default and should work well for queries that can be executed within a web request scope (<~1 minute)

Allow Run Async	☐

Allow users to run queries, against an async backend. This assumes that you have a Celery worker setup as well as a results backend.

Allow CREATE TABLE AS	☑

Allow CREATE TABLE AS option in SQL Lab

Allow DML	☑

Allow users to run non-SELECT statements (UPDATE, DELETE, CREATE, ...) in SQL Lab

CTAS Schema	CTAS Schema

When allowing CREATE TABLE AS option in SQL Lab, this option forces the table to be created in this schema

Impersonate the logged on user	☐

If Presto, all the queries in SQL Lab are going to be executed as the currently logged on user who must have permission to run them. If Hive and hive.server2.enable.doAs is enabled, will run the queries as service account, but impersonate the currently logged on user via hive.server2.proxy.user property.

Save ⬚ ←

Edit Database details form

Once you have created the `upload_csv` database integration, make sure you select it when you are uploading the `.csv` file, as shown in the following screenshot:

Load CSV form

Configuring the table schema

The **List Columns** tab on the **Edit Table** form lets you configure the **Column** attributes:

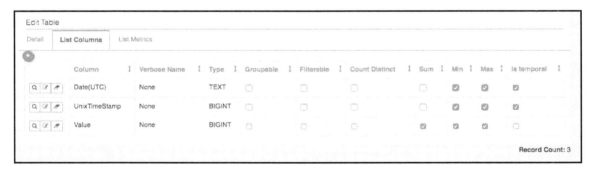

Edit column properties after adding a new table

Customizing the visualization

The Ethereum dataset has a **Date** (UTC) column, a **UnixTimestamp** column, and a value representing the total transaction volume in USD on that date. Let's chart the **Value** column in the latest Ethereum transaction history data:

Data form for the Ethereum transaction volume chart

The **Data** form calculates the sum of transactions grouped by dates. There is only one value over which the **SUM(Value)** aggregate function is computed:

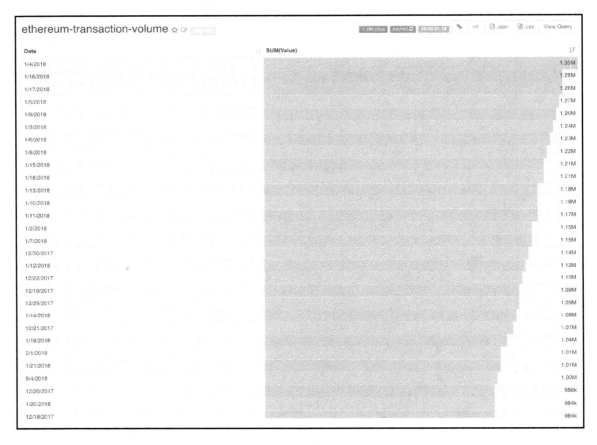

Table chart with total value of Ethereum over the years

The sum of transaction values, grouped by the **Date** column value and sorted in descending order, shows that the busiest days in the Ethereum network are also the most recent.

Making a dashboard

Making a dashboard in Superset is quick and easy. Just go to **Dashboards** and create a new dashboard. In the form, fill in the **Title** and a string value in the **Slug** field, which will be used to create the dashboard's URL, and hit **Save**:

Edit Dashboard form

Open the dashboard and select the **Edit Dashboard** option. Because we have two seemingly unrelated datasets, we can use the **Tabs** dashboard component to see them one at a time:

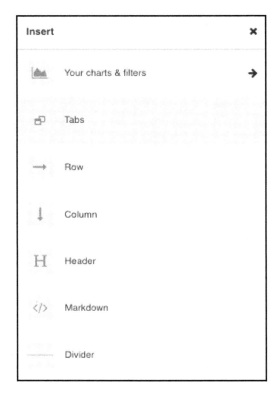

Insert components list when editing dashboard

Once you have added a **Tabs** component, insert the two charts you just made using the **Your charts & filters** option:

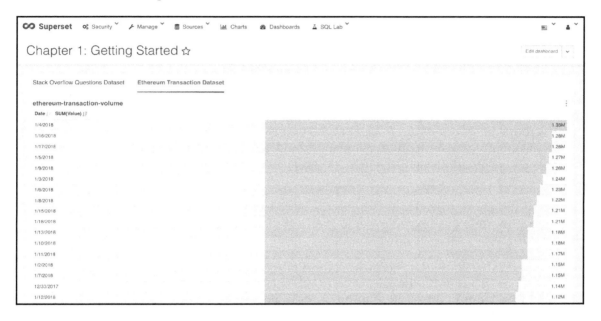

Dashboard for Chapter 1: Getting Started

The dashboard URL syntax is `http://{address}:{port number}/superset/dashboard/getting-started`. Replace the address and port number variables with the appropriate values, and you can use this link to open or share your dashboard.

Our dashboard is ready and live for users with accounts on the web server. In the next chapter, we will learn about user roles. After that, you will able to get your favorite collaborators to register. With them on board, you can start collaborating on charts and dashboards for your data analysis projects.

Summary

That must have felt productive, since we were able to create our dashboard from nothing in Superset.

Before we summarize what we have just finished in this chapter, it is important that we discuss when Superset might not be the right visualization tool for a data analysis project.

Visualization of data requires data aggregation. Data aggregation is a function of one or more column values in tables. A group by operation is applied on a particular column to create groups of observations, which are then replaced with the summary statistics defined by the data aggregation function. Superset provides many data aggregation functions; however, it has limited usability when hierarchical data aggregation is required for visualizations.

Hierarchical data aggregation is the process of taking a large amount of rows in a table and displaying summaries of partitions and their sub-partitions. This is not an option in Superset for most of the visualizations.

Also, Superset has limited customization options on the design and formatting of visualizations. It supports changes in color schemes and axis label formatting. Individuals or teams who want to tinker and optimize the visual representation of their data will find Superset very limited for their needs.

Finally, it's time to summarize our achievements. We have been able to install Superset, add a database, create a dashboard, and share it with users. We are now ready to add additional databases and tables, and create new visualizations and dashboards. Exploring data and telling data stories with Superset dashboards is one of your skill sets now!

2
Configuring Superset and Using SQL Lab

Superset has a flexible software architecture. This means that a Superset setup can be made for many different production environment needs. The production environment at Airbnb runs Superset inside Kubernetes and serves 600+ daily users, rendering over 100,000 charts every day.

At the same time, Superset can be set up with default settings for most users. When launching our first dashboard on a Google Compute Instance, we did not have to make any changes to the default parameters.

In this chapter, we will learn about the following:

- Setting the web server
- Metadata database
- Web server
- Setting up an NGINX reverse proxy
- Setting up HTTPS or SSL certification
- Flask-AppBuilder permissions
- Securing session data
- Caching queries
- Mapbox access token
- Long-running queries
- Upgrading Superset
- Main configuration file
- **SQL Lab**

Setting the web server

Start the Superset web server with this command:

```
superset runserver
```

Superset loads the configuration from a `superset_config.py` Python file. This file must be present in the path stored in the `SUPERSET_CONFIG_PATH` environment variable. The configuration variables present in this config file will override their default values. Superset uses the default values for variables not defined in the file.

So to configure the application, we need to create a Python file. After creating the Python file, we need to update `SUPERSET_CONFIG_PATH` to include the file path.

On your GCE instance, run the following commands:

```
shashank@superset:~$ touch $HOME/.superset/superset_config.py
shashank@superset:~$ echo 'export
SUPERSET_CONFIG_PATH=$HOME/.superset/superset_config.py' >> ~/.bash_profile
shashank@superset:~$ source ~/.bash_profile
```

Those are the last commands we will add to `.bash_profile`. `.bash_profile` must contain the following commands:

```
source /usr/local/bin/virtualenvwrapper.sh
export GOOGLE_APPLICATION_CREDENTIALS="$HOME/.google_cdp_key.json"
export SUPERSET_CONFIG_PATH=$HOME/.superset/superset_config.py
```

The `superset_config.py` file can also be used to configure the Flask backend. It is one of the components that Superset is built with. The configuration file can be used to alter Flask settings and Flask extensions such as `flask-wtf`, `flash-cache`, `flask-migrate`, and `flask-appbuilder`.

The configuration file with default values is present in the `Chapter02` directory of the GitHub repository; find it here: `https://github.com/PacktPublishing/Superset-Quick-Start-Guide/blob/master/Chapter02/superset_config.py`.

The `superset_config.py` Python file has many configurable parameters. We will understand the ones we need to make a production-ready Superset web server.

Creating the metadata database

The `SQLALCHEMY_DATABASE_URI` variable value is picked up by the Flask-AppBuilder manager to create the metadata database for the web app. The metadata database is persisted in `~/.superset/superset.db` by default. This can be verified by running `sqlite3` in the directory and listing the tables in the database:

```
shashank@superset:~/.superset$ sqlite3
SQLite version 3.16.2 2017-01-06 16:32:41Enter ".help" for usage
hints.Connected to a transient in-memory database.Use ".open FILENAME" to
reopen on a persistent database.
sqlite> .open superset.db
sqlite> .tables
ab_permission annotation_layer logs ab_permission_view clusters metrics
ab_permission_view_role columns query ab_register_user css_templates
saved_query ab_role dashboard_slices slice_user ab_user dashboard_user
slices ab_user_role dashboards sql_metrics ab_view_menu datasources
table_columns access_request dbs tables alembic_version favstar url
annotation keyvalue
```

Instead of SQLite, PostgreSQL or any other database can be used. To set up a production-ready Superset web server, we need to upgrade our metadata database to PostgreSQL. Installing PostgreSQL on a Google Compute Instance with Ubuntu, macOS, or any other Linux machine is straightforward.

First, we need the PostgreSQL and SQLAlchemy Python connector. In the virtual environment, we can install the required Python packages with this command:

```
shashank_f1@superset:~$ workon supervenv
(supervenv) shashank_f1@superset:~$ pip install psycopg2
```

On a Ubuntu OS, we need to install the following operating system libraries:

```
shashank@superset:~$ sudo apt-get -y install postgresql postgresql-client
postgresql-contrib
```

PostgreSQL creates a default user named `postgres` during installation:

```
(supervenv) shashank@superset:~$ sudo su postgres
postgres@superset:/home/shashank$ cd ~
```

Superset will require a database on the PostgreSQL installation to store its metadata. We will create a `superset` user role for Superset to access PostgreSQL, and secure it with a password:

```
postgres@superset:~/$ psql
postgres-# create database superset;
postgres-# CREATE USER superset WITH PASSWORD 'superset';
postgres-# GRANT ALL PRIVILEGES ON DATABASE "superset" to superset;
postgres-# \q
```

We need to configure PostgreSQL so that it uses md5 as the password authentication method. The Superset web server will use this protocol to authenticate with the metadata database. The `pg_hba.conf` file needs to edited to make this update:

```
postgres@superset:~$ vim /etc/postgresql/9.6/main/pg_hba.conf
# --- inside pg_hba.conf ---
# "local" is for Unix domain socket connections only
# local          all         postgres       peer
# replace with
local            all         postgres       md5
```

The PostgreSQL setup is complete! Now, we just need to restart it:

```
postgres@superset:~$ exit
(supervenv) shashank@superset:~$ sudo service postgresql restart
```

Finally, we know that we are ready to modify the SQLALCHEMY_DATABASE_URI variable. Let's assign it the SQLAlchemy URI for the PostgreSQL database that we just created:

```
# PostgreSQL URI format
# Syntax for a SQL Database URI
# SQLALCHEMY_DATABASE_URI =
"postgressql+psycopg2://<postgres_user>:<postgres_user_password>@localhost/
<postgres_database>"
SQLALCHEMY_DATABASE_URI =
"postgressql+psycopg2://superset:password@localhost/superset"
```

Because we moved the database variable from the default, SQLite, to PostgreSQL, we need to run a command to upgrade the database migration schemas and recreate the default metadata tables, this time in PostgreSQL. To do this, run the following:

```
(supervenv) shashank@superset:~$ superset upgrade
(supervenv) shashank@superset:~$ superset init
```

Migrating data from SQLite to PostgreSQL

Before we move forward, let's make sure all tables have been migrated from the SQLite database to the newly set up PostgreSQL database.

First, we need to migrate the SQLite metadata database to our new PostgreSQL installation. We will use `sequel`, an open-source database toolkit available as a Ruby gem. It works very well with migration tasks from `sqlite3` to PostgreSQL, which is why we are using it.

We will install OS dependencies and gem dependencies along with the `sequel` Ruby gem:

```
sudo apt-get install ruby-dev libpq-dev libsqlite3-dev
sudo gem install pg sqlite3
sudo gem install sequel
```

After installing `sequel`, the migration is as simple as running the following command. Make sure the path to the `sqlite3` database is set correctly:

```
sequel -C sqlite:///home/shashank/.superset/superset.db
postgresql://superset:superset@localhost/superset
```

We can log in to the PostgreSQL command-line console and list the metadata tables that have just been migrated:

```
psql -U superset
postgres-# \dt
                       List of relations
 Schema  |           Name            | Type  |  Owner
---------+---------------------------+-------+----------
 public  | ab_permission             | table | superset
 public  | ab_permission_view        | table | superset
 public  | ab_permission_view_role   | table | superset
 public  | ab_register_user          | table | superset
 . . .
```

Web server

We can integrate Superset with many web server options, such as Gunicorn, NGINX, and Apache HTTP, depending on our runtime requirements.

Web servers handle HTTP or HTTPS requests. A Superset web server typically processes a large number of such requests to render charts. Each request generates an I/O-bound database query in Superset. This query is not CPU-bound because the query execution happens at the database level and the result is returned to Superset by the database query execution engine. Requests to a Superset web server almost always require a dynamic output and not a static resource as a response. Gunicorn is a Python WSGI HTTP server. WSGI is a Python application interface based on the **Python Enhancement Proposal** (PEP) 333 standard. It specifies how Python applications interface with a web server. Gunicorn is the recommended web server for deploying a Superset web app.

Gunicorn

The Gunicorn web server is built to scale with increasing request loads. The master process creates child processes that handle each request. Another advantage is that when a request crashes, the master process remains unaffected. The forks are created before the request comes in. The number of worker processes can be set when Gunicorn is started. Four to twelve worker processes are able to handle thousands of requests per second. The operating system does the load balancing of the worker processes. The number of worker processes to use depends on the use case; it is recommended to start with (2x the number of CPU cores + 1) worker processes and then modify this based on production usage. There are two types of workers: sync and async, which handle one or many HTTP requests concurrently. Sync workers are suitable for CPU-bound processes. Async workers are recommended for I/O-bound processes. Requests to the Superset app will mostly be I/O-bound via database connection pools, where it will submit data read requests. So, in the case of Superset, we will configure Gunicorn to use the gevent Python library implementation of async workers.

In order to use Gunicorn, we need to install the gevent Python concurrent worker library in Superset's virtual environment:

```
(supervenv) shashank@superset:~$ pip install gunicorn gevent
```

After installation, when we run gunicorn, we can provide configuration parameters to gunicorn to match our performance needs, like in the following example:

```
export SUPERSET_UPDATE_PERMS=0
gunicorn -w 3
 -k gevent
 --timeout 120
 -b 0.0.0.0:8088
 superset:app
```

The arguments used in the command are described here:

Argument	Description	Value
w	Number of concurrent workers	3
k	worker_class	gevent
timeout	Time threshold in seconds after which silent workers are killed and restarted	120
b	Bind address	0.0.0.0:8088
app	Python app name	superset

In cases where clients or Superset web app users have very slow internet connections, it is preferable to setup Gunicorn behind NGINX, Apache HTTP, or an AWS Elastic Load Balancer.

Setting up an NGINX reverse proxy

We are going to set up NGINX as a proxy server that will retrieve resources on behalf of a client from the Gunicorn web server. NGINX has many functionalities and it is the most popular proxy server in use. We will use it primarily to redirect connections when someone enters a registered web domain name in their web browser, or the external IP address directly into our Superset web server.

We will set up SSL certification for the NGINX proxy server. This way, web connections to our web app will always be encrypted and secure. More popular browsers, such as Chrome and Firefox, will show a warning if the web page does not have an SSL certificate. No worries, we will get the certificate!

We will first install NGINX in our GCE instance. GCE runs an Ubuntu OS:

```
# Install
sudo apt-get update
sudo apt-get install nginx
```

The NGINX service is now installed in the Ubuntu OS, and we are running it as a service. When using Superset's **Upload a CSV**, it is possible that we might have to upload large files. To avoid a HTTP Request Entity Too Large error, which NGINX reports with uploaded file objects greater than 1 megabyte, we will make one change to NGINX's configuration file.

Open the file:

```
sudo vim /etc/nginx/nginx.conf
```

Then, insert or update this attribute inside the `http` scope:

```
http {
 ....
 client max body size 50M;
 ...
}
```

After saving the configuration file, let's reload NGINX:

```
# Start and Reload
sudo nginx -s start sudo nginx -s reload # Check status systemctl status
nginx
```

Let's create the configuration file NGINX will use for forwarding connections to the Superset server:

```
# -- inside superset.conf --
# save in /etc/nginx/sites-enabled/

server {
 listen 80;
 # you need to modify this value
 # to the external ip or web domain of
 # the machine
 server_name 35.233.249.126;
 root /var/www/superset;
 location / {
 proxy_buffers 16 4k;
 proxy_buffer_size 2k;
 proxy_pass http://127.0.0.1:8088;
 proxy_set_header Host $http_host;
 }
}
```

The `listen 80` statement tells NGINX to listen on port 80. Port 80 is the default port where browsers send connection requests for HTTP/HTTPS connections. The server name is the external IP address of the GCE instance you are using.

Note that under the `location/` field in the file, we are configuring NGINX to route server name requests to localhost and port 8088, where the Gunicorn server is accepting connection requests.

Finally, let's create a link between this configuration file and the sites-available NGINX module:

```
sudo ln -s /etc/nginx/sites-available/superset.conf /etc/nginx/sites-enabled
```

We will restart the NGINX server after compiling the configuration file for errors:

```
# test for syntax errors
sudo nginx -t
# reload
sudo nginx -s reload
```

Setting up HTTPS or SSL certification

We will be using Let's Encrypt (https://letsencrypt.org/) a free, automated, and open certificate authority managed by the non-profit **Internet Security Research Group (ISRG)**.

Secure Socket Layer (**SSL**) is a secure transport layer that can be used in any protocol; HTTPS is a common instance of it, that we will be implementing for our Superset web server.

Just like most other things, configuring SSL has OS level dependencies. First, we will install certbot, which is the free automated certificate service. It needs to verify our site first. It does this by doing some checks (which it calls challenges) in http://<url>/.well_known:

```
# Install certbot
sudo add-apt-repository ppa:certbot/certbot
sudo apt-get install certbot

# Create .well_known directory
cd /var/www/html
mkdir .well_known
```

We also need to update the superset.conf file in the sites-available directory to redirect connection requests to url/.well_known to the empty .well_known directory, which letsencrypt will use for running challenges:

```
# superset.conf
# save in /etc/nginx/sites-enabled/

server {
```

```
            listen 80;
            server_name 35.233.249.126;
            root /var/www/superset;
            location / {
                proxy_buffers 16 4k;
                proxy_buffer_size 2k;
                proxy_pass http://127.0.0.1:8088;
            }
            location /.well-known {
                alias /var/www/html/.well-known;
            }
    }
```

We will run the `certbot` application with the `webroot` plugin. Once it finishes the challenges successfully, it will get a certificate:

```
certbot certonly --webroot -w /var/www/35.233.249.126 -d 35.233.249.126
```

Note that we are using the external IP as the URL or web address for our Superset application. If you have a domain name registered, you can also replace the server name value in the `superset.conf` file and the value next to the `-d` flag with the registered domain name instead of the external IP as the URL for the Superset web app.

The certification process will ask for the following:

- Your email address.
- Agreement on a terms of service.
- Domains for which HTTPS will be available.
- Whether to redirect HTTP to HTTPS. It is recommended that HTTP is redirected to HTTPS.

It will detect the list of domains mentioned in the server name field in the file linked to sites-enabled. If the certification process is successful, you should be able to verify it by listing the files inside `/etc/letsencrypt/live/` followed by the server name directory:

```
shashank@superset:~$ sudo ls /etc/letsencrypt/live/35.233.249.126/
cert.pem chain.pem fullchain.pem privkey.pem README
```

The SSL certificates expire after a fixed time period. The `certbot renew` command attempts to renew any previously obtained certificates that expire in fewer than 30 days. We can configure `renew-hook` so that, when certbot renews certificates successfully, it also restarts NGINX:

```
shashank@superset:~$ certbot renew --renew-hook "sudo  nginx -s reload"
```

Whenever the certificate expires, we have to run this command to renew the certificate. We can set that up as a regularly scheduled job by adding a line to `crontab`, which is available by default in the Ubuntu OS:

```
shashank@superset:~$ crontab -e

# Add this line to renew >30day certs everyday at 12pm
0 12 * * * certbot renew --quiet --renew-hook "sudo nginx -s reload"
```

That was a lot of work but now the Superset web server can accept HTTPS connections, which makes the production-ready server a bit more secure!

Flask-AppBuilder permissions

Superset uses the Flask-AppBuilder framework to store metadata required for permissions in Superset. Every time a Flask-AppBuilder app is initialized, permissions and views are automatically created for the **Admin** role. When multiple concurrent workers are started by Gunicorn, they might lead to contention and race conditions between the workers trying to write to one metadata database table.

The automatic updating of permissions in the metadata database can be disabled by setting the value of the `SUPERSET_UPDATE_PERMS` environment variable to zero. It is one or enabled by default:

```
export SUPERSET_UPDATE_PERMS=1 superset init
# Make sure superset init is called before Superset starts with a new
metadata database
export SUPERSET_UPDATE_PERMS=0 gunicorn -w 10 ... superset:app
```

Securing session data

Session data that is exchanged between the Superset web server and a browser client or internet bot can be encrypted using the `SECRET_KEY` parameter value present in the `superset_config.py` file. It uses a cryptographic one-way hashing algorithm for encryption. Since the secret is never included with data the web server sends to a browser client or internet bot, neither can tamper with session data and hope to decrypt it.

Just set its value to a random string of length greater than ten:

```
SECRET_KEY = 'AdLcixY34P' # random string
```

Caching queries

Superset uses Flask-Cache for cache management and Flask-Cache provides support for many backend implementations that fit different use cases.

Redis is the recommended cache backend for Superset. But if you do not expect many users to use your Superset installation, then **FileSystemCache** is a good alternative to a Redis server.

The following are some of the cache implementations that are available, with a description and their configuration variables:

CACHE_TYPE	Description and configuration
simple	Uses a local Python dictionary to store results. This is not really safe when using multiple workers on the web server.
filesystem	Uses the filesystem to store cached values. The CACHE_DIR variable is the directory path used by FileSystemCache.
memcached	Uses a memcached server to store values. Requires the pylibmc Python package installed in the virtual environment: pip install pylibmc. The CACHE_MEMCACHED_SERVERS variable is the list or a tuple of memcached server addresses.
saslmemcached	Uses a memcached server with a SASL-enabled connection to store values. pylibmc is required and SASL must be supported by libmemcached. Just like MemcachedCache, it requires pylibmc and libmemcached to support SASL: pip install pylibmc, pip install libmemcached. For Ubuntu, there are two additional OS dependencies: sudo apt-get install libmemcached-dev and sudo apt-get install libz-dev. CACHE_MEMCACHED_USERNAME is the username to use for SASL authentication with memcached. CACHE_MEMCACHED_PASSWORD is the password to use for SASL authentication with memcached.

spreadsaslmemcached	This is the same as MemcachedCache with the additional ability to spread a value across multiple keys if it is bigger than the memcached threshold, which by default is 1M. It uses the pickle Python package for data serialization.
redis	Uses a Redis server to store values. CACHE_REDIS_HOST is the Redis server host. CACHE_REDIS_PORT is the Redis server port. The default value is 6379. CACHE_REDIS_PASSWORD is the Redis password for the server. CACHE_REDIS_DB is the index number for the Redis database (zero-based number index). Default is 0. CACHE_REDIS_URL is the URL to connect to Redis server, for example, redis://user:password@localhost:6379/2.

The CACHE_KEY_PREFIX prefix in CACHE_CONFIG is appended to all keys stored in the cache implementation. This makes it possible to use the same memcached server for different apps.

We will use the recommended Redis cache backend for our Superset running on the GCE.

Let's then install Redis in the Ubuntu OS:

```
shashank@superset:~/$ sudo apt-get install redis-server
# restart redis server
shashank@superset:~/$ sudo systemctl restart redis-server.service
# enable start on reboot
shashank@superset:~/$ sudo systemctl enable redis-server.service
```

Without a Redis configuration file, the default SQLAlchemy URI for the server is redis://localhost:6379/0. In the Superset configuration file, we will set the CACHE_CONFIG variable value to select this running Redis cache server:

```
CACHE_CONFIG = {
  # Specify the cache type
  'CACHE_TYPE': 'redis',
  'CACHE_REDIS_URL': 'redis://localhost:6379/0',
  # The key prefix for the cache values stored on the server
  'CACHE_KEY_PREFIX': 'superset_results'
}
```

Mapbox access token

The `MAPBOX_API_KEY` variable needs to be defined because we will use Mapbox visualizations in Superset charts. We need to get a Mapbox access token using the guidelines available here: `https://www.mapbox.com/help/how-access-tokens-work/`.

After you have obtained it, set the `MAPBOX_API_KEY` variable to the valid access token value.

Long-running queries

Database queries that are initiated by Superset to render charts must complete within the lifetime of HTTP/HTTPS requests. Some long-running database queries can cause a request timeout if they exceed the maximum duration of a request. But it is possible to configure Superset to handle long-running queries properly using a Celery distributed queue, and transfer the responsibility of query handling to Celery workers.

In large databases, it is common to run queries that run for minutes and hours while most commonly web request timeouts are within 30-60 seconds. Therefore, it is necessary that we configure this asynchronous query execution backend for Superset.

We need to ensure that the worker and the Superset server both have the same values for common configuration variables.

Redis is the recommended message queue for submitting new queries to Celery workers. So, we will use our already running Redis server in our Celery configuration:

```
class CeleryConfig(object):
    BROKER_URL = 'redis://localhost:6379/0'
    CELERY_IMPORTS = ('superset.sql_lab', )
    CELERY_RESULT_BACKEND = 'redis://localhost:6379/0'
    # Rte limit new long queries to 10 per second
    CELERY_ANNOTATIONS = {'tasks.add': {'rate_limit': '10/s'}}

CELERY_CONFIG = CeleryConfig
```

Celery workers also require a results backend for persisting asynchronously returned query results. In the configuration file, we need to set the `RESULTS_BACKEND` variable. For this, we will also need to import a `RedisCache` class using an `import` statement inside the `superset_config.py` file:

```
from werkzeug.contrib.cache import RedisCache
RESULTS_BACKEND = RedisCache(host='localhost',
```

```
port=6379,
key_prefix='superset_results')
```

Main configuration file

So, we have completed configuring Superset. Let's take a look at the complete Superset configuration file:

```
# Superset Configuration file
# add file superset_config.py to PYTHONPATH for usage

# Metadata database
SQLALCHEMY_DATABASE_URI =
"postgresql+psycopg2://superset:superset@localhost/superset"

# Securing Session data
SECRET_KEY = 'AdLcixY34P' # random string

# Caching Queries
CACHE_CONFIG = {
 # Specify the cache type
 'CACHE_TYPE': 'redis',
 'CACHE_REDIS_URL': 'redis://localhost:6379/0',
 # The key prefix for the cache values stored on the server
 'CACHE_KEY_PREFIX': 'superset_results'
}

# Set this API key to enable Mapbox visualizations
MAPBOX_API_KEY = os.environ.get('MAPBOX_API_KEY', 'mapbox-api-key')

# Long running query handling using Celery workers
class CeleryConfig(object):
BROKER_URL = 'redis://localhost:6379/0'
CELERY_IMPORTS = ('superset.sql_lab', )
CELERY_RESULT_BACKEND = 'redis://localhost:6379/0'
 # Rte limit new long queries to 10 per second
CELERY_ANNOTATIONS = {'tasks.add': {'rate_limit': '10/s'}}

CELERY_CONFIG = CeleryConfig

# Persisting results from running query handling using Celery workers
from werkzeug.contrib.cache import RedisCache
RESULTS_BACKEND = RedisCache(host='localhost',
port=6379,
key_prefix='superset_results')
```

We just need to check that the file is present in the SUPERSET_CONFIG_PATH environment variable before we run our Superset web server:

```
(supervenv) shashank@superset:~$ echo $SUPERSET_CONFIG_PATH
/home/shashank_f1/.superset/superset_config.py
```

Let's open a new ssh Terminal for the Gunicorn web server. We will run the Gunicorn web server with 10 workers and a HTTP/HTTPS timeout of 120 seconds on port 8088:

```
source ~/.bash_profile
export SUPERSET_UPDATE_PERMS=0
gunicorn -w 10 -k gevent --timeout 120 -b 0.0.0.0:8088 superset:app
```

In another new Terminal, for long-running queries, let's start celery worker, which will use the same metadata database as the Superset web server:

```
celery worker --app=superset.sql_lab:celery_app --pool=gevent -Ofair
```

Great! We have five running services currently on the Superset production server:

- PostgreSQL database for handling concurrent queries to the metadata database (running as a background service):

  ```
  sudo service postgresql restart
  ```

- Redis server for caching query results and persisting results for long-running queries (running as a background service):

  ```
  sudo systemctl restart redis-server.service
  ```

- NGINX (running as a background service):

  ```
  sudo nginx -s reload
  ```

- Superset running on a Gunicorn web server (running on a Terminal):

  ```
  gunicorn -w 3 -k gevent --timeout 120 -b 0.0.0.0:8088 superset:app
  ```

- celery worker (running on a Terminal):

  ```
  celery worker --app=superset.sql_lab:celery_app --pool=gevent -
  Ofair
  ```

That is a good setup for a Superset production server!

Let's get back to data exploration now that we are finally done configuring Superset.

Just use the server name you listed in your NGINX `superset.conf` configuration file as the URL for the internet browser. It will be either the instance's external IP or a registered domain name you may have linked to the external IP.

If you do not want the NGINX reverse proxy setup, you can continue to use the external IP with the `8088` port number as the URL for accessing Superset. If you are running Superset in a private network, then you should have an internal IP but the same `8088` port number.

We have finally arrived at the home screen of the configured Superset web app:

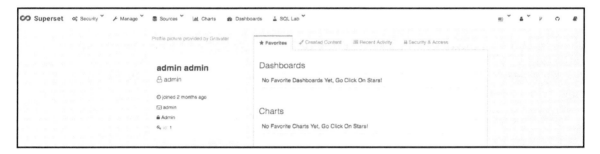

Home screen of the configured Superset web app

SQL Lab

SQL Lab is a powerful SQL IDE inside Superset. It works with any database that has a SQLAlchemy Python connector. It is great for data exploration. It can query any data sources in the Superset, including the metadata database.

It is a solid playground from which we can slice and dice the dataset in many ways to arrive at a form that needs to be visualized to solve the analytical question that the chart was created to answer.

First, we need to enable **SQL Lab** use on the `superset-bigquery` data source. We will explore and visualize the data in the table using SQL queries.

After clicking on the **Sources** | **Databases** option on the navigation bar, select the **Edit record** option for the `superset-bigquery` data source:

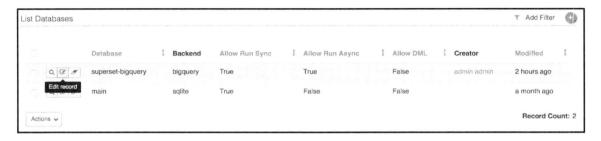

The overview chart of the list of databases

Then, make sure the following three options are enabled. **Allow Run Sync** should be enabled by default. We are doing this to use the data source in **SQL Lab** and also to allow Celery workers to execute queries on it. Save the changes when you are done and we will next add a new table to Superset:

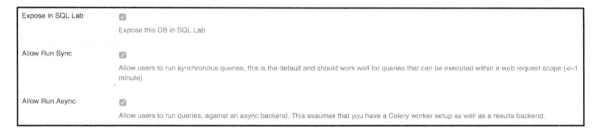

The `HackerNews` dataset in the `bigquery` data source contains all stories, comments, jobs, and polls from Hacker News since its launch in 2006. There are five types of record in the dataset: story, comment, job, poll, or pollopt. Each record has attributes that have a null or non-null value based on their type. Records of type story have a unique ID, the author of the post, a timestamp for when it was written, and the number of points the story received. Let's start exploring this data; just select the **SQL Lab** button on the navigation bar and then select **SQL Editor**:

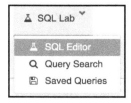

When you open **SQL Editor**, the metadata database named main will already selected. When you also select the schema as main, the table drop-down list will give you one of 32 table options to select.

Change the drop-down option to `superset-bigquery`. It is possible that no schemas or tables are listed. No worries! Just use the **SQL Editor** to look up and query the table. Use this SQL code to select and print 10 rows from the table:

```
SELECT
    *
FROM
        `bigquery-public-data.hacker_news.full`
LIMIT 10;
```

The output of the preceding query is as follows:

Overview of sample rows from the table

We can see a sample of the rows from the table. I am genuinely curious as to the properties of stories that trend on Hacker News. Stories that accumulate many points tend to trend higher. Just to do something simple, let's look at which URL domains are most popular in the dataset.

To do this, we will open a new tab and query to print the top domains, sorted by the number of stories that link to them:

Query to print the top domains

Well, looks like `https://github.com/` and `http://medium.com` are very popular websites on Hacker News. Perhaps, comparing the points to the top two URLs accumulating in posts over time will be useful. This can used to find whether GitHub or Medium has done consistently better over time. They both have a similar number of stories. There are 3911 more posts from `https://github.com/`, or 5.7% more than the number of posts from `http://medium.com`.

So in this query result, points from stories are summed up within groups defined by URL domain and month. If you want to get this query again later, or share this result with someone else, there are a few options.

One option is to save this query. It is a good idea to specify details about the query in the description section:

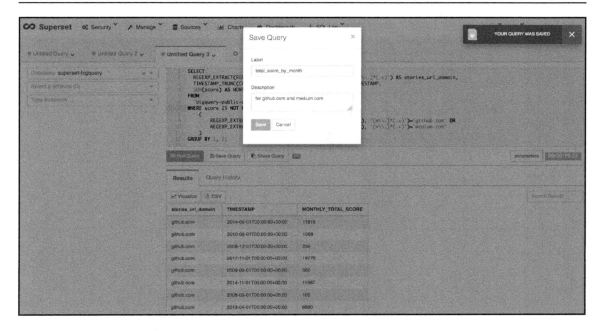

Labeling and adding a description of the query to save

Later, anyone with **SQL Lab** access can use the **Saved Queries** option in the **SQL Lab** drop-down option list to check out saved queries:

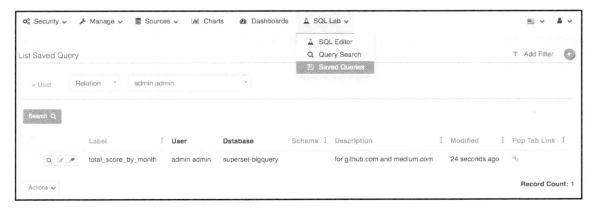

Option to view queries that are saved

```
SELECT
    REGEXP_EXTRACT(REGEXP_EXTRACT(url,'[a-z]+://([^/]+)/'), '[w\\.]*(.+)') AS
stories_url_domain,
```

```
    TIMESTAMP_TRUNC(CAST(timestamp AS TIMESTAMP), MONTH) AS TIMESTAMP,
    SUM(score) AS MONTHLY_TOTAL_SCORE
FROM
    `bigquery-public-data.hacker_news.full`
WHERE score IS NOT NULL AND type='story' AND
    (
        REGEXP_EXTRACT(REGEXP_EXTRACT(url,'[a-z]+://([^/]+)/'),
'[w\\.]*(.+)')='github.com' OR
        REGEXP_EXTRACT(REGEXP_EXTRACT(url,'[a-z]+://([^/]+)/'),
'[w\\.]*(.+)')='medium.com'
    )
GROUP BY 1, 2;
```

To look up previously run queries, we can check out the **SQL Editor** query logs available in the **Query Search** option:

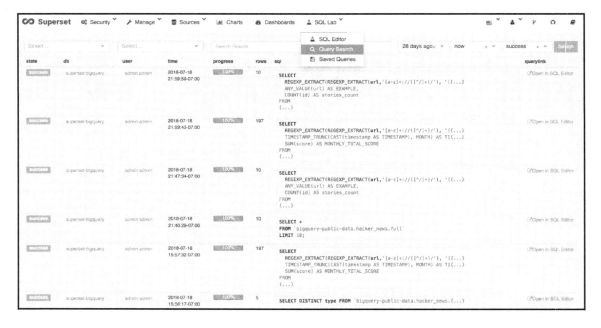

Overview of the Query Search option

Okay, we have saved our query and also parameterized it. Now, let's visualize it! Just click the **Visualize** option over the results table to make a chart using the results data. It will open a configuration box, where we can specify that we want to plot a line plot over time instead of the default bar chart:

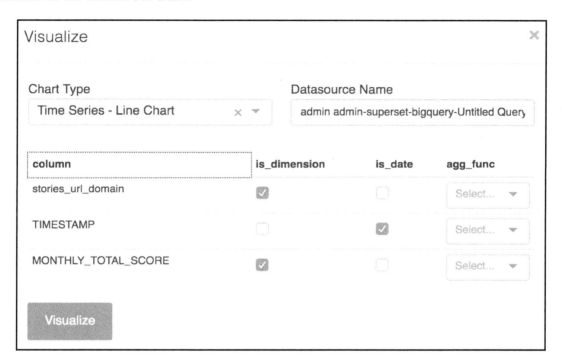

Even though we are not using any granular time grains, we have to select an **agg** function for the **MONTH_TOTAL_SCORE** that we want to plot. So, let's plot the aggregate function as **SUM** and name it. This is the value plotted on the *y* axis, which also sets the same name as **MONTHLY_TOTAL_SCORE**:

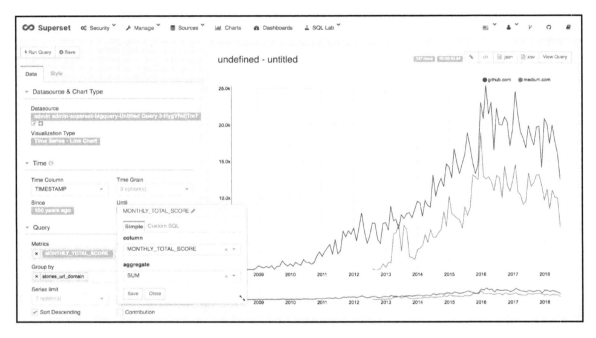

Chart based on the result of the data

Finally, we can make a conclusion from that chart. Hacker News posts from `https://github.com/` have always accumulated more points over monthly time periods than posts from `http://medium.com`. And, there is a small difference (5%) in the number of Hacker News posts, at 72080 and 68169 for `https://github.com/` and `http://medium.com` respectively.

Summary

We understood that when the Superset web server is started we can configure it for our runtime environment needs using the `superset_config.py` file. We looked at the configuration parameters that can make Superset secure and scalable to match optimal trade-offs.

SQL Lab provides an opportunity to experiment with result sets before plotting. It can be used as an excellent tool for exploring datasets and developing charts.

In this chapter, we replaced SQLite metadata with a PostgreSQL database and configured a web app to use it as the database. So that the web app can handle many concurrent users, we deployed it on a Gunicorn server:

- PostgreSQL metadata database
- Gunicorn
- NGINX
- HTTPS authorization
- Securing session data
- Redis caching system
- Celery for long-running queries
- Mapbox access token

Nicely done! We have been able to make dashboards, use **SQL Lab**, and understand the various configuration parameters required to optimize Superset for our use case. You can now set up your own production-ready Superset web server. Let's move forward in our Superset journey.

3
User Authentication and Permissions

Superset's user management is defined using roles. Roles are templates of permission sets that can be applied on one or more users, and modified if required. They can be used to manage permissions for different types of Superset user. Data analysts might need permissions to build new charts and modify data sources, but some users might only need permissions to view specific dashboards. Separate user roles have to be applied to both types of user.

Alpha and gamma are the building blocks of user roles. With either of those templates, we can assign a custom set of permissions and save it as a new role. We can then create roles such as data analyst, DevOps engineer, business, and product manager and apply them to one or many users.

The `superset init` command that was executed to set up Superset synchronizes the definition of roles such as alpha and gamma, and a list of web app permissions. Access control is made up of permissions and parts of the web app that can be accessed. In Django terminology, these parts or rendered pages of a web app are call views. The values for these objects are initialized or reset in the metadata database every time the `init` command is run.

In this chapter, we will learn about the following:

- Security features
- Setting up OAuth Google sign-in
- **List Users** page
- **List Base Permissions** page
- **Views/Menus** page
- List Permissions on **Views/Menus** page

- Alpha and gamma—building blocks for custom roles
- **User Statistics** page
- Action log

Security features

Access to security features in Superset is available only to the admin user. It provides several tools for tracking every user action, login attempt, a list of users, and their permissions.

The user management system is built using the Flask-AppBuilder (`fabmanager`) framework. The list of permissions and views is inherited from the Flask-AppBuilder framework. Permissions and views are listed in the **Views/Menus** page of the **Security** section. A view represents many ways a user can interact with the web application. Each user has a specific set of permissions for actions that it can take when interacting with a web page or view. Viewing or deleting a dashboard are examples of actions.

Setting up OAuth Google sign-in

Flask-AppBuilder supports many authentication protocols. The default database authentication protocol allows the creation of new users by the admin. When creating the user, the admin sets a default password and shares it with the users along with their username. However, this is quite a cumbersome way to onboard new collaborators to your Superset web app.

The OAuth protocol allows the use of external authorization services such as Google, Facebook, and Twitter. Once any of these OAuth services are put in place, users can register and sign in themselves, without requiring any action by the admin. We will change the default database-based authentication to Google OAuth.

In the `superset_config.py` file, we can whitelist a set of emails that can register and log in to the web app. Suffix patterns can be used to allow all email addresses with the same suffix, such as `@apache.org`.

Before we modify the `superset_config.py` file to switch to Google OAuth, we have to register our application on the Google **APIs & Services** console. Go to `https://console.developers.google.com/apis/dashboard` and select **Credentials** from the left pane:

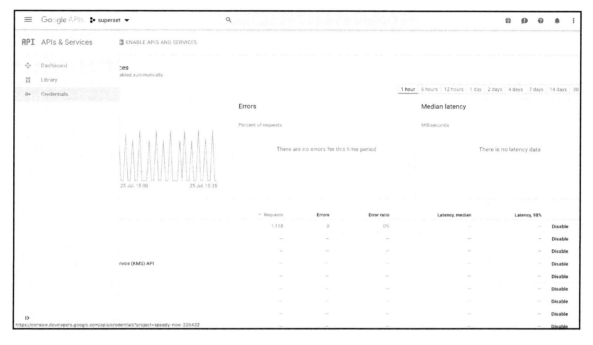

Application registration on Google APIs & Services

In the **Credentials** section, click on **Create credentials** and select **OAuth client ID**:

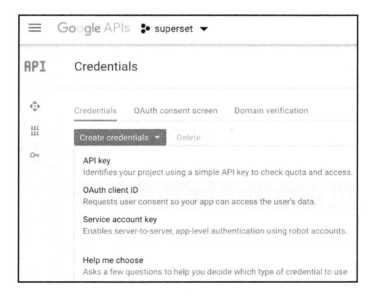

Next, you will see the **Create OAuth client ID** form, where you need to insert a **Name** for the web application. In the following screenshot, I have set the name as `superset-quick-start`:

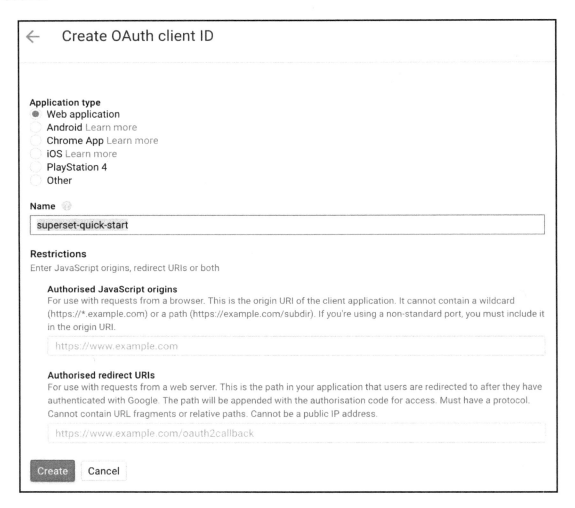

On the **APIs & Services** dashboard, OAuth 2.0 client IDs will be listed after creation. When you click on the application name in the list, it will show the client ID and client secret. We will need both of them to integrate Superset authentication with Google OAuth. Use the **Download JSON** option on the **Client ID** page to save the contents in the home directory of the GCE instance.

The OAuth configuration file should look like this:

```
shashank@superset:~$ cat /.google_oauth_key.json
{
    "web":{
        "client_id":"<client-id>",
        "project_id":"<project-id>",
        "auth_uri":"https://accounts.google.com/o/oauth2/auth",
        "token_uri":"https://accounts.google.com/o/oauth2/token",
"auth_provider_x509_cert_url":"https://www.googleapis.com/oauth2/v1/certs",
        "client_secret":"<client-secret>"
    }
}
```

In .bash_profile, we need to create an environment variable named GOOGLE_OAUTH_CREDENTIALS. This will store the path of the credentials file. After adding the environment variable, your .bash_profile should like this:

```
export SUPERSET_CONFIG_PATH=$HOME/.superset/superset_config.pysource
/usr/local/bin/virtualenvwrapper.sh
export MAPBOX_API_KEY="<your-mapbox-api-key>"
export GOOGLE_APPLICATION_CREDENTIALS="$HOME/.google_cdp_key.json"
export GOOGLE_OAUTH_CREDENTIALS="$HOME/.google_oauth_key.json"
```

Before we update the superset_config.py file, remember to execute the bash_profile file in the current shell:

```
shashank@superset:~$ source ~/.bash_profile
shashank@superset:~$ echo $GOOGLE_OAUTH_CREDENTIALS
/home/shashank/.google_oauth_key.json
```

We also need to install a Python package required for Flask-AppBuilder to use the OAuth protocol for authentication:

```
pip install Flask-OAuthlib
```

Well, that finishes the environment setup for using Google OAuth on Superset. There are two values that have to be updated in the configuration file. One is the email address whitelist and the second is the role that we will assign to new users who registered using their Google account.

Because we need an admin account, we will first register a user with an Admin role, then later on change the value to Alpha. The following are the new configuration variables for the superset_config.py file:

```
from flask_appbuilder.security.manager import AUTH_OAUTH
import json

CSRF_ENABLED = True
AUTH_TYPE = AUTH_OAUTH
AUTH_USER_REGISTRATION = True
# Role assigned to new authorized and registered users
AUTH_USER_REGISTRATION_ROLE = "Admin"
auth_credentials =
json.load(open(os.environ.get('GOOGLE_OAUTH_CREDENTIALS')))['web']
OAUTH_PROVIDERS = [
        {
            'name': 'google',
            # email whitelist
            'whitelist': ['shashank@packtpub.com'],
            'icon': 'fa-google',
            'token_key': 'access_token',
            'remote_app': {
                'base_url': 'https://www.googleapis.com/oauth2/v2/',
                'request_token_params': {
                    'scope': 'email profile'
                },
                'request_token_url': None,
                'access_token_url': auth_credentials['token_uri'],
                'authorize_url': auth_credentials['auth_uri'],
                # google api & services client id and secret
                'consumer_key': auth_credentials['client_id'],
                'consumer_secret': auth_credentials['client_secret']
            }
        }
    ]
```

Once you have added these values to the file, and made sure whitelist only specifies your Gmail ID, restart the Superset web server and the celery worker on two new Terminals:

```
# Terminal 1
gunicorn -w 3 -k gevent --timeout 120 -b 0.0.0.0:8088 superset:app
#Terminal 2
celery worker --app=superset.sql_lab:celery_app --pool=gevent -Ofair
```

The following is how your `superset_config.py` file should look at this point:

```python
# Superset Configuration file
# add file superset_config.py to PYTHONPATH for usage
import os
import json
from flask_appbuilder.security.manager import

# Metadata database
SQLALCHEMY_DATABASE_URI =
"postgresql+psycopg2://superset:superset@localhost/superset"
# Securing Session data
SECRET_KEY = 'AdLcixY34P' # random string
# Caching Queries
CACHE_CONFIG = {
 # Specify the cache type
 'CACHE_TYPE': 'redis',
 'CACHE_REDIS_URL': 'redis://localhost:6379/0',
 # The key prefix for the cache values stored on the server
 'CACHE_KEY_PREFIX': 'superset_results'
}
# Set this API key to enable Mapbox visualizations
MAPBOX_API_KEY = os.environ.get('MAPBOX_API_KEY')
# Long running query handling using Celery workers
class CeleryConfig(object):
 BROKER_URL = 'redis://localhost:6379/0'
 CELERY_IMPORTS = ('superset.sql_lab', )
 CELERY_RESULT_BACKEND = 'redis://localhost:6379/0'
 # Rate limit new long queries to 10 per second
 CELERY_ANNOTATIONS = {'tasks.add': {'rate_limit': '10/s'}}

CELERY_CONFIG = CeleryConfig

# Persisting results from running query handling using Celery workers
from werkzeug.contrib.cache import RedisCache
RESULTS_BACKEND = RedisCache(host='localhost', port=6379,
key_prefix='superset_results')

# Google OAUTH Secrets
CSRF_ENABLED = True
AUTH_TYPE = AUTH_OAUTH
AUTH_USER_REGISTRATION = True
AUTH_USER_REGISTRATION_ROLE = "Admin"
auth_credentials =
json.load(open(os.environ.get('GOOGLE_OAUTH_CREDENTIALS')))['web']
OAUTH_PROVIDERS = [
 {
 'name': 'google',
```

```
'whitelist': ['shashank@packtpub.com'],
'icon': 'fa-google',
'token_key': 'access_token',
'remote_app': {
'base_url': 'https://www.googleapis.com/oauth2/v2/',
'request_token_params': {
'scope': 'email profile'
},
'request_token_url': None,
'access_token_url': auth_credentials['token_uri'],
'authorize_url': auth_credentials['auth_uri'],
'consumer_key': auth_credentials['client_id'],
'consumer_secret': auth_credentials['client_secret']
}
}
]
```

Just head over to the external IP of the machine on your browser, select **G**, and click
Register:

Congratulations! You should have signed in to your Superset web app now using Google sign in. The new account will have the admin role assigned to it, which means you should have permissions to view and access the **Security** section. On the **List Users** page, your new account will be listed. Because only your Google email is whitelisted in the `superset_config.py` file, no one else can register on your server. We will change this after understanding how to define new roles for users.

List Users page

Admins have access to the **Security** section. As an admin, you will be able to access this page in the **Security** drop-down. It is a tool for editing permissions and roles assigned to any user. The admin has all the permissions, including the ability to alter users, data sources, charts, and dashboards. When new users register, they will appear on this page. Users with admin privileges can alter the permissions and roles for new users.

List Base Permissions page

This page has a list of permissions that can be applied on a view or menu. The current user has the admin role so has all the permissions on all the **Views/Menus** items in the Superset web app. The admin role and gives permission to alter all charts, dashboards, data sources, and users. Gamma roles do not have permissions to alter any charts, dashboards, data sources, or users. But we can create customized roles that are assigned the gamma role with additional permissions on specific data sources. This will allow the new custom role to view charts on permitted data sources. They also have permission to create new charts on those data sources.

The alpha role gives permissions to view all charts and dashboards, alter all charts and dashboards, and alter data sources, but not to modify permissions for other users:

Views/Menus page

This page lists all **Views/Menus** available in the Superset web app. Admin users can assign permissions specific to each **Views/Menus**. In most production setups, fine-grained permissions for **Views/Menus** are not required:

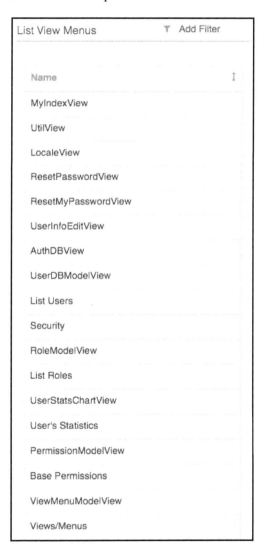

List Permissions on Views/Menus pages

This page lists permissions, with the **Views/Menus** on which they can be used. When it is necessary to assign finer-grained permissions in customized user roles, this is a useful page from which to look up permissions:

List Permissions on Views/Menus	▼ Add Filter
Permission	**View/Menu**
can_this_form_post	ResetPasswordView
can_this_form_get	ResetPasswordView
can_this_form_post	ResetMyPasswordView
can_this_form_get	ResetMyPasswordView
can_this_form_post	UserInfoEditView
can_this_form_get	UserInfoEditView
can_edit	UserDBModelView
can_userinfo	UserDBModelView
can_delete	UserDBModelView
can_download	UserDBModelView
can_list	UserDBModelView
can_add	UserDBModelView
can_show	UserDBModelView
resetmypassword	UserDBModelView
resetpasswords	UserDBModelView
userinfoedit	UserDBModelView
menu_access	List Users
menu_access	Security
can_edit	RoleModelView

Alpha and gamma – building blocks for custom roles

We will manage user permissions using alpha, gamma, and customized roles. In `superset_config.py`, only one email ID should be whitelisted for registration. We will need more Google accounts to register for testing different permissions. You can put in any regex pattern in the `whitelist` field. Suffixes such as `@amino.com` are commonly used to allow users from a specific email domain to register on the web app. If a Google account email address matches the pattern specified in `whitelist`, it will be able to register itself.

We will modify `superset_config.py` so that a Google account with any email can register. Moving forward, new users will be assigned a `Gamma` role with no default permissions on any data source. In order to do that, we will modify two lines in the file:

```
# Modification 1
# Assigns Gamma role for new registered users
AUTH_USER_REGISTRATION_ROLE = "Gamma"
auth_credentials =
json.load(open(os.environ.get('GOOGLE_OAUTH_CREDENTIALS')))['web']
OAUTH_PROVIDERS = [
        {
            'name': 'google',
            # Modification 2
            # Commented to allow any email to register
            # 'whitelist': ['shashank@packtpub.com'],
            ...
```

After saving the configuration file, you will have to restart the Gunicorn web server and Celery workers to load the new version.

Alpha

The alpha role is for users who need permissions to add or alter tables in any databases. It is suitable for users who want to create new tables, charts, and dashboards. Only admin users have the ability to add databases. Some users will need access to **SQL Lab** for developing new analytics, so a user with the alpha role also needs to be assigned the sql_lab role. Admin users have access to **SQL Lab**.

On a separate browser, log in with a new Google account. This is a good time to ask a collaborator who will use your Superset setup to register with their Google account. New users will not have permissions to view any tables, charts, or dashboards:

Gamma users do not have access to SQL Lab

After they have registered, log in with your account, which has the admin role. We will remove the gamma role auto-assigned to the new registered user and replace it with **Alpha** and **sql_lab** user roles. You can do this by going to **Security I List Users**. Search for the new user's record and select **Edit Record**. Remove the assigned gamma role and replace it with **Alpha** and **sql_lab** roles:

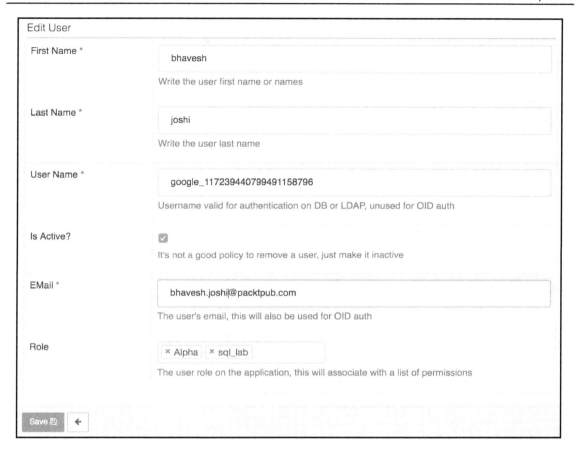

When the new user logs back in, they will have permissions to view all existing data sources, charts, and dashboards. **SQL Lab** will now also appear in the top navigation bar:

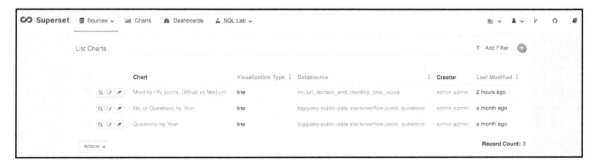

Existing data sources, charts, dashboards, and SQL Lab now available to the new user

Gamma

The gamma role is for users who need permissions to view and create charts and dashboards.

These users will need customized roles that give them read permissions on data sources. Data source access only gives them view permissions on charts and dashboards, without any ability to alter them. But, they can create new charts for permitted data sources.

We will test out a combination of page Gamma role with data source access permissions. Go to **List Roles** | **Add Role** and create a customized user role with a permission to access the `bigquery-public-data.stackoverflow.posts_questions` data source:

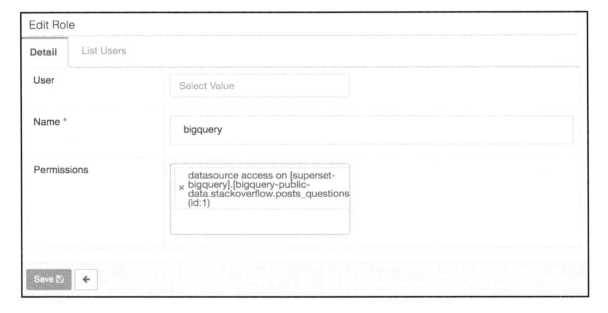

Next, go to **List Users** and select the new user, and go to **Edit Record**. Then, remove the **Alpha** and **sql_lab** roles, replace them with the **Gamma** and **bigquery** roles, and perform a **Save**:

When the user logs back in, they will no longer have permissions to view any charts and dashboards, alter data sources, or use **SQL Lab**. They will be able to view charts and dashboards that use a data source they have been given access to in the **bigquery** role. In the following screenshot, you can see that only charts that use the `bigquery-public-data.stackoverflow.posts_questions` data source are now listed:

Public

Public is the role used for unregistered users. By default, the public role has no permissions. Users cannot even view a list of databases that are accessible to users with only the `Gamma` role. It is not recommended that you provide any permissions to the `Public` role.

For quick reference, the following table describes each role, broken down by types of functions they can perform:

	Admin	Alpha	Gamma	SQL Lab
Add or remove users	Yes	No	No	No
Create, remove, or modify data sources	Yes	Yes	No	No
View charts and dashboards	Yes	Yes	Yes, if data source access also available	No
Modify charts and dashboards	Yes	Yes	No	No
Create charts and dashboards	Yes	Yes	Yes, if data source access assigned and also available	No
SQL Lab access	Yes	No	No	Yes

User Statistics page

This page shows the number of logins grouped by the registered username. This is a useful tool for admins to track usage. Administrators can use the filters in the following chart to see login counts for different sets of users:

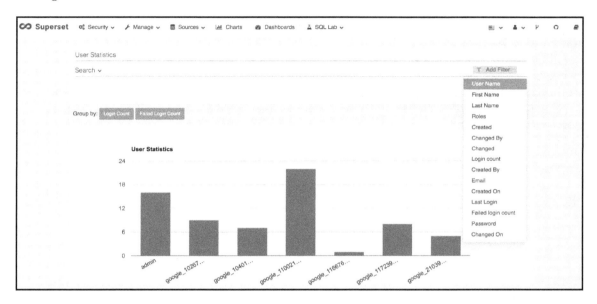

Logins grouped by registered username

Action log

This page lists the activity for all registered users. This is a useful tool for monitoring user activity. Logs can be filtered by **User**, **Action**, **Dashboard Id**, **dttm**, and other fields:

Activity for all registered users

Summary

That's a wrap! We figured out how to allow new users to register on the Superset web app with their Google account. The OAuth configuration can be extended to provide users with Facebook, Twitter, or GitHub accounts to also register and sign in easily. We explored many security tools available to the administrator, such as activity logs and **User Statistics**. Our current setup will support user management for collaborators who will need Alpha roles and **SQL Lab** access, so that they can add or alter data sources, make new charts, and dashboards, or work in **SQL Lab**. Using the gamma role and data source access permissions, supports use cases for users who will only need to interpret charts and dashboards on specific data sources. For example, people in the finance team may only need the ability to view charts on finance-related data sources, while data analysts may need access to add new data sources and create dashboards.

In this chapter, we learned about security and permissions, covering the following important topics:

- Google OAuth
- Permissions
- User roles
- Action log

In the next chapters, we will build a variety of charts such as scatter plot, sunburst, and heatmaps among others using new data sources.

Visualizing Data in a Column

4

Tabular data is present everywhere! And for most analytics, answers are available in a few important columns. Tables can have many columns, but some columns are more significant than others. Each column in a tabular dataset represents a unique feature of the dataset. Once we have identified a column of interest, our goal in this chapter is to make visualizations in Superset that help us to explore and interpret that data.

In this chapter, we will understand columnar data through distribution plots, a point-wise comparison with reference columns, and charts that are just one-line summaries:

- **Distribution**: Histogram
- **Comparison**: Distribution box plots for subsets of column values
- **Comparison**: Compare distributions of columns with values belonging to different scales
- **Comparison**: Compare metrics and distributions between subsets of column values
- **Summary statistics**: Headline

Dataset

A favorite on my blogroll at `https://austinrochford.com/` is a good place to discover intuitive explanations of Bayesian machine learning methods. In the December 29, 2017 blog post *Quantifying Three Years of Reading* (`https://austinrochford.com/posts/2017-12-29-quantifying-reading.html`), the blogger analyzes changes in their own reading log dataset. The reading log is available as a Google sheet at this link: `https://docs.google.com/spreadsheets/d/1wNbJv1Zf4Oichj3-dEQXE_lXVCwuYQjaoyU1gGQQqk4/`.

The reading log is a time series dataset, which the blogger frequently updates. I have taken a snapshot of the reading log and saved it in the chapter's GitHub directory, `https://github.com/PacktPublishing/Superset-Quick-Start-Guide/Chapter04/`. The dataset has been modified by the addition of a new column. You can run the Jupyter Notebook `generate_dataset.ipynb` to generate the dataset on your own.

Once you upload the CSV, you can open the **List Columns** tab to confirm that all column names and types are correctly represented as follows:

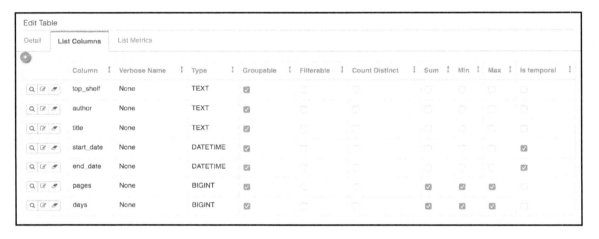

Column attributes for the austinrochford.com modified reading log dataset

Distribution – histogram

After uploading the file as a table, open it for visualization and select the **Histogram** option. Make sure that **start_date** is selected as **Time Column**. The **Time** window defined between **Since** and **Until** must be large enough to include all the books, because we do not want to do any **Time** window-specific analysis.

Page count is an important feature in the dataset, where each row is a book. It is a numerical value. So, to begin with let's look at a distribution plot of page counts. It will give us a sense of the variance in the feature value:

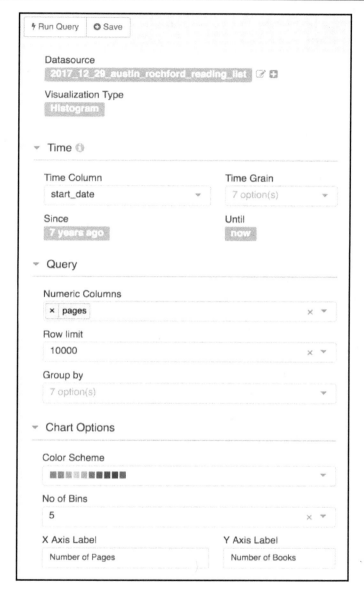

Data form for a histogram chart

The number of bins in a histogram limits the granularity of questions we can answer about the variance of the feature:

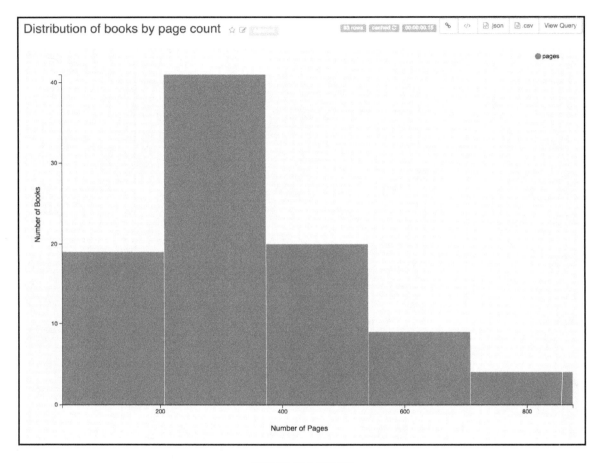

Distribution plot of page counts

Because we have set five bins, what is identifiable is that about 41-42 out of 93 books (approx. 44%-45%) have page counts of between **200** and **400**. More bins can help discover smaller dominant feature ranges. When samples within a bin are not uniformly distributed, the true variance can only be understood by breaking down the bin into multiple bins representing smaller ranges.

Comparison – relationship between feature values

Let's say we are curious about a trend where the time taken to read a book increases with respect to the page count.

Books often have a gripping effect on a reader, once they find them interesting. So, we cannot expect the number of pages to proportionately grow with the number of days taken to read a book, because books that the reader finds gripping will be read at a faster pace than others. In any dataset, there are samples that are noisy and hard to explain. In this dataset, we will find that some books with lower page counts take more days to finish than books with higher page counts.

It will be useful to look at the number of samples we have available for each group, defined by number of reading days. Select **COUNT(*)** as **Metrics** to plot the **number_of_books** read:

Defining the reading capacity for each group of books

We will get the following output:

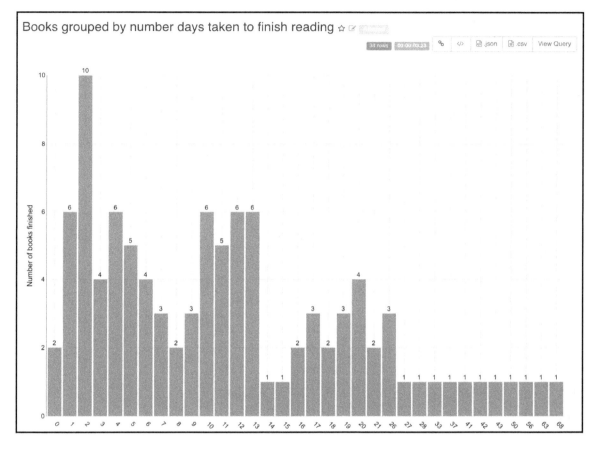

Number of books finished in x number of days

Now, let's choose a different metric for the *y* axis. Instead of plotting the count, plot the minimum page count of the books grouped by reading days. The idea behind selecting this metric is that the lowest page count also the most slowly read book in its group, since all books in the group were read in the same number of days:

Plotting the minimum page count in books grouped by days

Based on our previous chart, we know that there is only one sample for reading days greater than or equal to 27. We can see that the smallest page count for each group increases gradually with an increase in the number of days for the 1 to 26 *x* axis range:

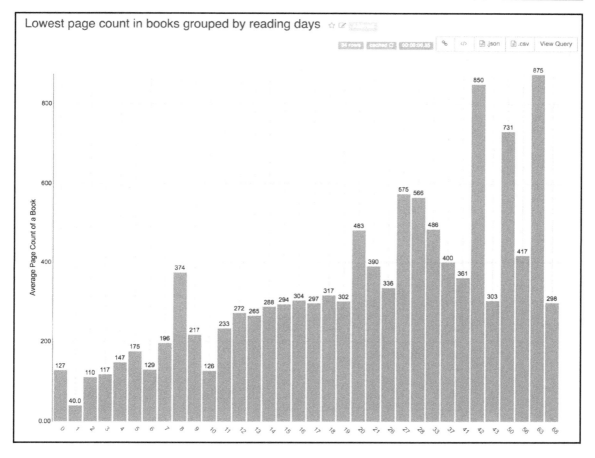

Lowest page count in books grouped by reading days

Comparison – box plots for groups of feature values

The previous charts described the relationship between days taken to finish reading a book and page count. Now, we will try to understand the highest page counts in calendar months, where a book was finished after x number of reading days. In the first chart, we plotted the number of samples we have for each group of books, which were completed in the same number of days. There are multiple samples in many groups. Here, we will plot a distribution for multiple samples in each group.

We can define a statistic to summarize the average page counts of books completed in the same calendar month as the a book was completed after x number of days.

We will make a box plot chart as follows:

Parameters to set box plot chart

The data that we are visualizing in this box plot is made using multiple group by operations, because the box plots shows median and other percentiles, look at the following chart:

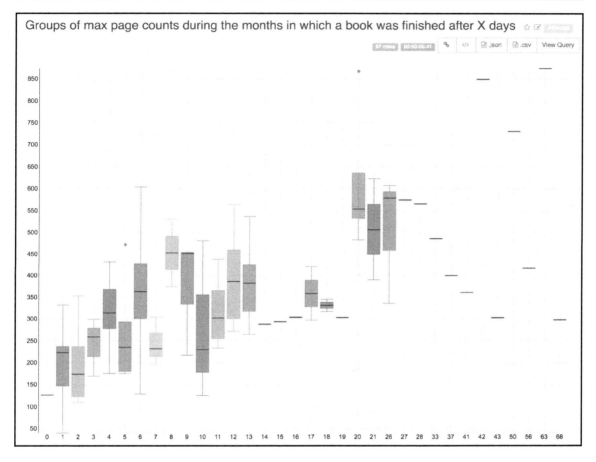

Box plot made by using multiple group by operations

It is a good idea to look at the transformed data and then interpret this chart. Let's use the **Export to .csv format** option available in the top right. It will download the CSV locally on the machine where you are accessing your Superset web app:

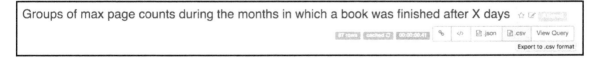

Export to CSV option available

Sort the CSV by **days** and **_timestamp** to see the values plotted in each of the boxes:

days	_timestamp	SUM(pages)
0	2018-02-01	127
1	2016-05-01	40
1	2018-04-01	147
1	2017-06-01	223
1	2018-05-01	237
1	2018-06-01	474
2	2018-01-01	110
2	2017-01-01	114
2	2017-10-01	126
2	2016-07-01	165
2	2015-05-01	236
2	2018-06-01	353
2	2018-08-01	355
2	2018-05-01	450

Days and timestamp of the boxes

Comparison – side-by-side visualization of two feature values

With a time series dataset, interactions can best be analyzed by plotting two features side by side on a shared **Time** axis. Let's say we are curious to ascertain how, on a monthly basis, the page count of books affects the number of books read that month. To do this, we will use **Dual Axis Line Chart**. To mark the books finished on the **Time** axis, select **end_date** as the **Time Column** and **month** as the **Time Grain**. We select the page count of the longest book read and the number of books read for each month as follows:

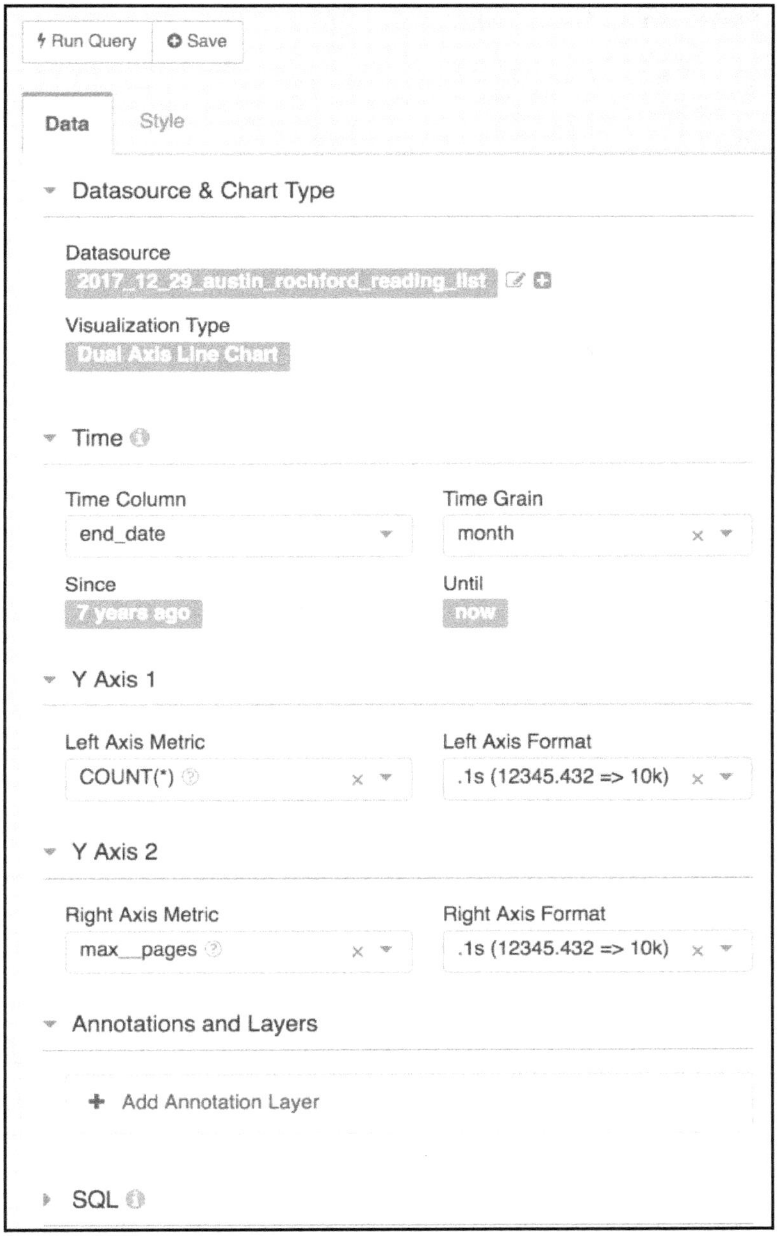

⚡ Run Query   ⊕ Save

Data   Style

▾ Datasource & Chart Type

Datasource
2017_12_29_austin_rochford_reading_list ☑ ➕

Visualization Type
Dual Axis Line Chart

▾ Time ⓘ

Time Column   Time Grain
end_date   ▾   month   × ▾

Since   Until
7 years ago   now

▾ Y Axis 1

Left Axis Metric   Left Axis Format
COUNT(*) ⓘ   × ▾   .1s (12345.432 => 10k)   × ▾

▾ Y Axis 2

Right Axis Metric   Right Axis Format
max__pages ⓘ   × ▾   .1s (12345.432 => 10k)   × ▾

▾ Annotations and Layers

✚ Add Annotation Layer

▸ SQL ⓘ

Setting the parameters for two feature values

The output for it is displayed as follows:

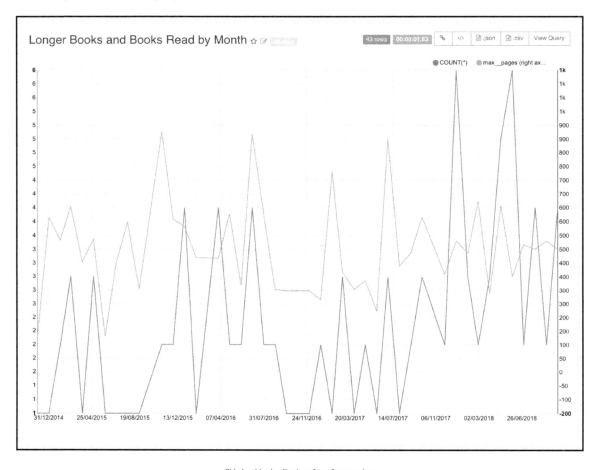

Side-by-side visualization of two feature values

It is noticeable that the two *y* axes have repeated values. The range of the left *y* axis value is 1 to 6, and the range of the right axis value is 100 to 900. Additionally, in the 3 months of October 2015, May 2016, and May 2017, the blogger finished one to three other books.

Summary statistics – headline

Superset has a chart useful for dashboards called a headline. It is a chart that plots a single metric. Single numbers can answer key questions that we have about datasets.

In the process of analyzing the page count feature using charts in Superset, we looked at its distribution and its relationship with other features. One of the simplest questions one can ask is the average number of days required to read per page.

We will plot the average value for the page count divided by days across all books to capture the answer to that question. In Superset, we can write **Custom SQL** code to calculate metrics:

Customizing SQL code to calculate a metric

After clicking on the **Metric**, select the **Custom SQL** tab to write **AVG(pages/days)** as the code:

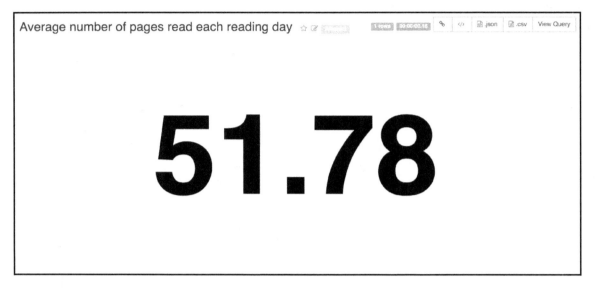

Average number of pages read each reading day

Information in charts must be easy to understand. The precision of the decimal number seems like extra information that may not be as useful:

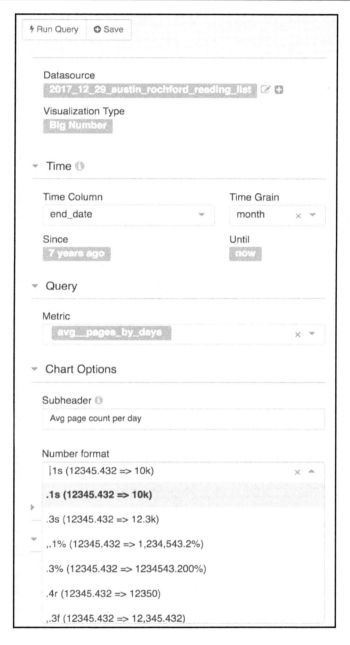

Limiting the precision of the metric

We can use the **Number format** option to limit the precision of the metric, and, using the **Subheader** option, we can insert some large text into our chart:

Subheader option used to enlarge the text

This will explain clearly what that number represents. Now, the chart is easier to understand.

Summary

That completes our exploration of the page count feature value. By compiling those charts, we have aggregated sufficient charts to make a dashboard that anyone who has questions about the page count feature of the dataset will find useful. In the next chapter, we will compile charts with a view to understanding the relationship between two different feature values instead of just focusing on one.

5
Comparing Feature Values

Given a table with many columns, an understanding of the range and simple statistics of the feature values in every column often results in an individual becoming curious about how different features affect one another. Relationships between features are modeled as correlation measures. Formulating and computing correlations between features in a dataset is a complex problem. Sometimes, joint distribution plots are able to encapsulate and visualize these relationships very well.

We can visualize multiple features for every row at once as points on a chart. The bubble chart in Superset can be used to visualize a feature type on the y axis perpendicular to the x axis timeline. A second feature is color-coded, and a third feature value is reflected as bubble size in a group of one or more rows in a dataset. In this chapter, we will make the following charts:

- A multiple line chart against a time x axis differentiated by color-coding
- An area chart against a time x axis differentiated by color-coding
- A bubble chart
- A dual axis line chart
- A time series percentage change

There are other charts that reflect the relative percent change for each time step. A rose chart displays the feature value distributed over arcs on concentric circles, so that you can visually compare across multiple features. There are effective charts for feature comparison available in Superset that are not used in this chapter. Do explore other charts with your own datasets so that you can develop intuition for selecting charts.

In this chapter, we will specifically cover the following, using a time series dataset:

- Comparing multiple time series
- Comparing two time series
- Identifying differences in trends for two feature values

Dataset

We will be working with trading data on commodities in this chapter. The Federal Reserve Bank of St Louis, United States, compiles data on commodities. Datasets are available on http://fred.stlouisfed.org. You can obtain time series data on import values and import volumes of commodities traded by the United States. We will download data on bananas, olive oil, sugar, uranium, cotton, oranges, wheat, aluminium, iron, and corn.

Inside the chapter directory of the GitHub repository, you will find the generate_dataset.ipynb Jupyter Notebook. Just run the Notebook to download, transform, and generate the two CSV files we will upload. If you want to skip running the Notebook, the two CSV files, fsb_st_louis_commodities.csv and usda_oranges_and_bananas_data.csv, are also present in the repository, ready for upload.

The FSB data on commodity prices in fsb_st_louis_commodities.csv was collected between 1980 and 2017.

The USDA trade data on oranges and bananas will be used to perform a deeper analysis of the prices. It introduces a new feature—import volume, with which we will compare import prices. The import value and import volume data in usda_oranges_and_bananas_data.csv covers the time period between January 2014 and September 2016. The data that we need is a subset of the data that is publicly available on the USDA website. You can download the TradeTables Excel file for oranges from this link: https://data.ers.usda.gov/reports.aspx?programArea=fruitstat_year=2009top=5HardCopy=TrueRowsPerPage=25groupName=CitruscommodityName=OrangesID=17851:

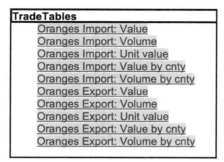

Trade tables data for oranges

You will find additional tables in the Excel file, which we will not be analyzing in this chapter.

When uploading the fsb_st_louis_commodities.csv file, we have to specify **DATE** as the temporal column. Values in the **DATE** column are in **DD-MM-YY** format. The temporal column in the second CSV file, usda_oranges_and_bananas_data.csv, is named timestamp. When uploading the usda_oranges_and_bananas_data.csv CSV file, timestamp has to be specified in the **Parse Dates** field. We don't need to specify the format for both the CSV files. Superset uses pandas to automatically interpret temporal data stored in different formats:

Parse Dates	
	timestamp
	A comma separated list of columns that should be parsed as dates.

Parse Dates fields updated with the timestamp

Comparing multiple time series

The time series line chart is useful for visualizing the price trends for every type of commodity together. Using the first dataset that was uploaded, we will visualize prices of commodities over time on the *x* axis and see how they compare against each other, as follows:

Setting the parameters for the time series chart

Remember to clear the time thresholds in the **Time** section. Then, select **feature** as the **Group by** value, **AVG(value)** as **Metrics**, and render the graph:

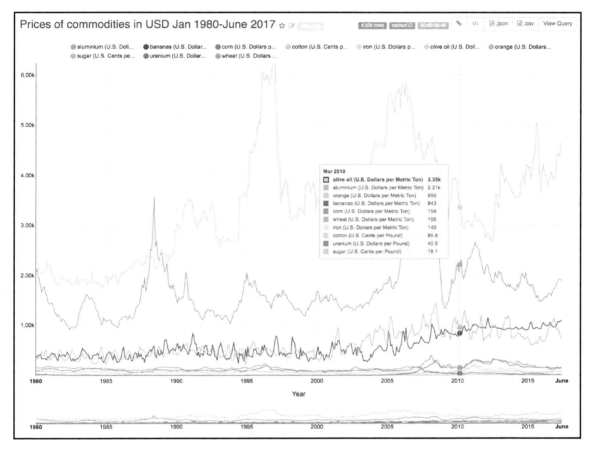

The time series line chart for all values

The tooltip shows the *y* axis price values for each commodity type and the units used. We can notice that the highly priced commodities have mostly non-overlapping price ranges. The data extends from January 1980 to June 2018. After the expensive commodities, bananas and oranges have fairly overlapping price ranges. It will be easier to compare values when they are observed within smaller ranges. So, let's hide all the series, except bananas and oranges:

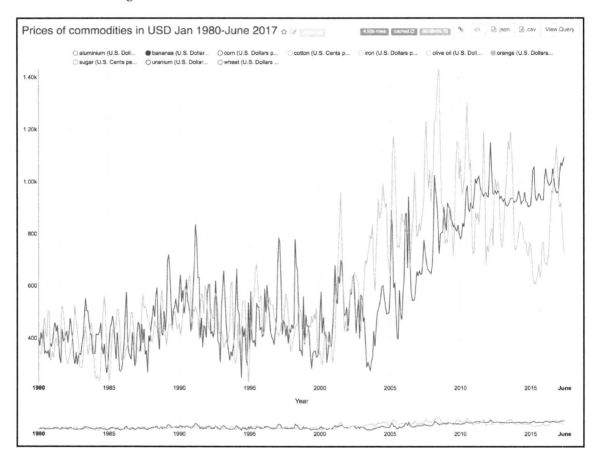

The time series line chart for some values

We can see that the two commodities also share a similar major upward trend in the last decade. Orange prices in the global commodity market have a much higher variance than banana prices over the last few years.

Comparing two time series

Stacked charts are often useful for measuring the combined area covered and relative differences in *y* axis values for two or more series. We will use the time series stacked chart to compare the prices of oranges and bananas:

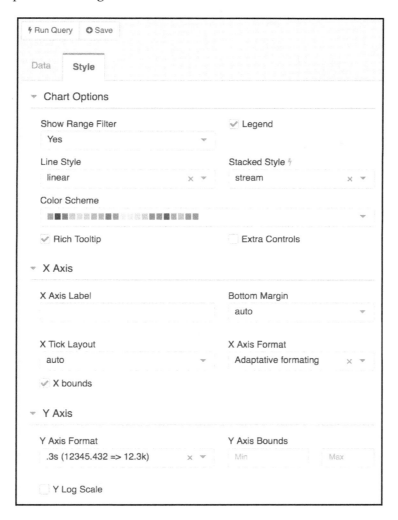

Setting parameters for the time series stacked chart

The **Style** section of the chart provides a **stream** style option. The width of each stream is proportional to the value in that category:

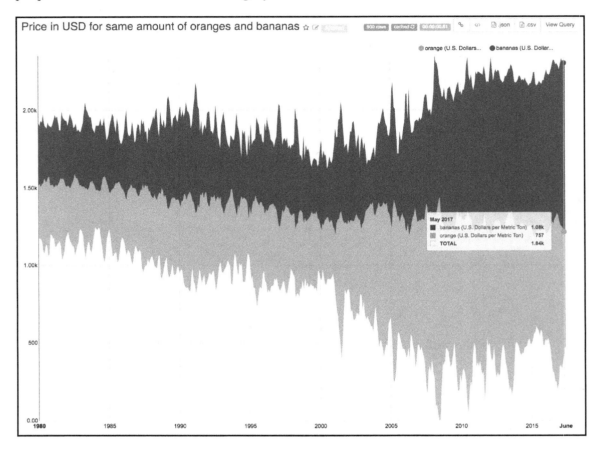

Time series stacked chart

In the stacked chart, the increase in price of both bananas and oranges is visualized through the increasing width of the stream. Since 2010, the color-coded streams show that oranges have had a relatively higher price variance than bananas. We can switch to expand styles and see whether, besides the higher price variation, oranges show a higher upward trend in prices:

Changing the variation

After switching to expand style, it is noticeable that oranges have tended to be more expensive than bananas during some time periods, but they are not always more expensive than bananas:

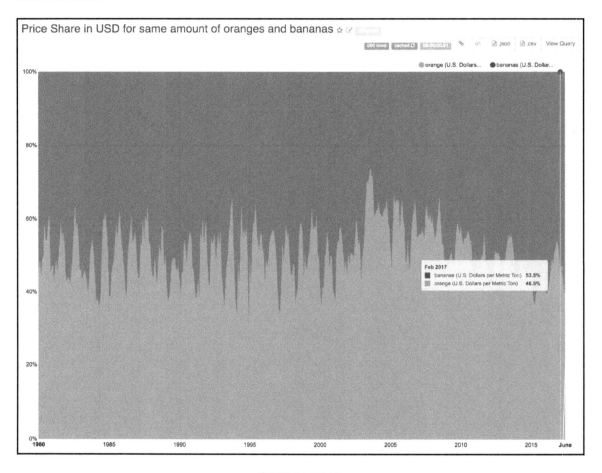

Switching to expand style

Identifying differences in trends for two feature values

Bananas are a year-round fruit. By comparison, oranges are harvested from December to June. Perhaps the seasonality of oranges has something to do with the higher price variation. The second dataset that we uploaded has values and volumes of oranges imported in different forms, such as `fresh oranges`, `orange juice`, and `preserved oranges`:

Running the query for extracting the data of oranges imported in different forms

In the **SQL Editor** inside **SQL Lab**, I wrote a query to list the different forms of oranges. We can focus on the effect of seasonality by only selecting `fresh oranges` and `fresh bananas` in subsequent charts.

We will make a bubble chart to compare the import value of oranges to bananas. Bubble charts also support visualization of a third data dimension using **Bubble Size**. Since we are interested in comparing the import value of oranges to bananas, let's set the size of the bubbles relative to the import value of oranges, divided by the import value of bananas, over a month:

Setting values of the bubble chart

You can see the output as follows:

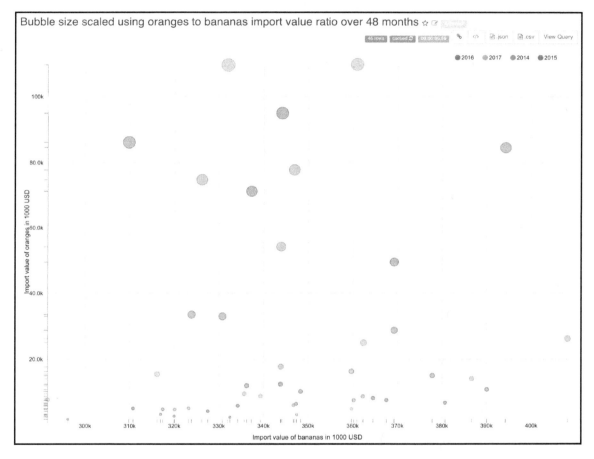

The bubble chart

The bubble charts looks pretty! The larger bubbles are rising to the top, associated with months that reported very high orange import values. The smaller bubbles are distributed across the *x* axis, but they are similarly concentrated near months with low orange import values.

In the bubble chart, the two largest bubbles each year are either August or July. On the flip side, November and December are the months where the smallest bubbles are made. Perhaps we can gain some insight by comparing import values and volumes for oranges. The months of July and August might also report higher import volumes.

A comparison of two feature types, one in USD 1,000 units and the other in 1,000 pound units, can be done using **Dual Axis Line Chart** as follows:

Setting values for a dual axis line chart

The output will be as follows:

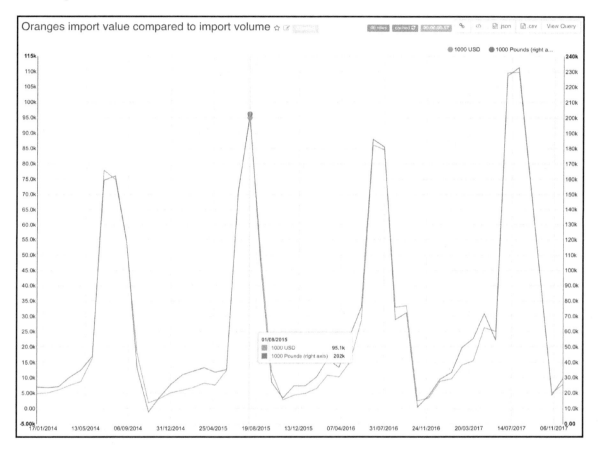

Dual axis line chart

Hovering over the curve shows that in the months of July and August, both import volumes and values increase significantly for the 3 years' worth of data. We can compare import values and volumes for bananas to see any effect of seasonality on the two time indexed features:

Setting values for a dual axis line chart

The output can be shown as follows:

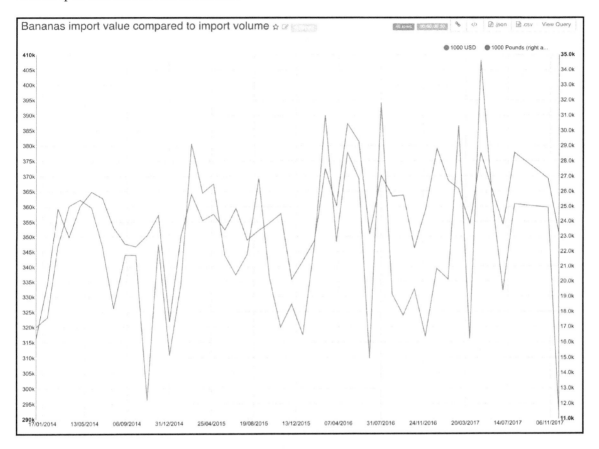

Dual axis line chart

Neither of the two banana features seem to show characteristic dips or slows in any specific month. After comparing the prices of oranges and bananas, we were able to establish that oranges have a higher price variation over time, even though oranges and bananas are generally similarly priced. We had a glimpse of the mechanics of the price variation by noting the higher import volume and, consequently, the import value, in the months of July and August for oranges. And bananas, by comparison, do not show any periodicity in import volume and value relative to specific months.

We will visualize our finding about the higher price variation in oranges using data from the second CSV file. We will make a chart showing a percentage change over time in the import value and import volume equal to import price in USD per pound for the two fruits:

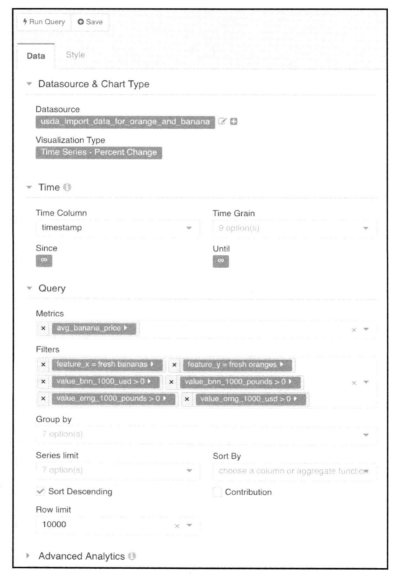

Setting values for the percentage factor of the price variation in bananas

The output can be shown as follows:

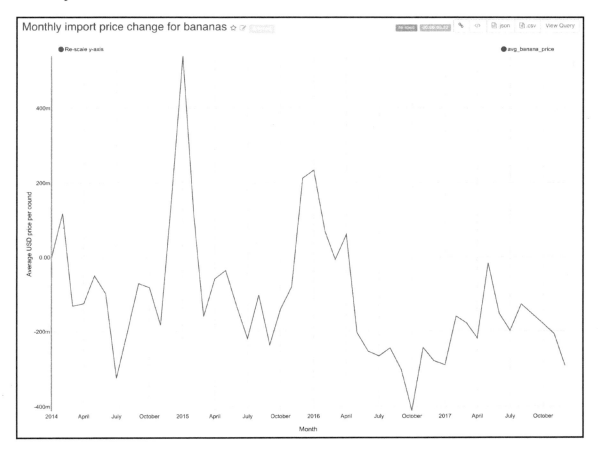

Monthly import price change as a percentage for bananas

The import data from 2014-2017 shows only 3 months in which prices increased by over 20% in successive months. The percentage change chart as regards the import value and volume data of oranges tells a different story, however:

Setting values for the percentage factor of the price variation in oranges

The output can be displayed as follows:

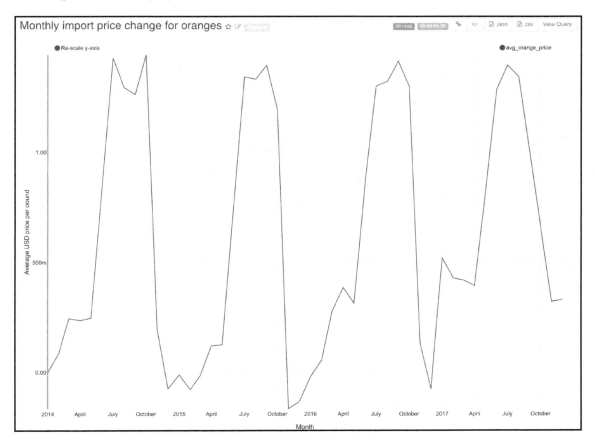

Monthly import price change as a percentage for oranges

In the dual axis line chart, we saw that import volumes grew with import values in the months of July and August. Using the time series percentage change chart to compare relative price differences between subsequent months, it is easy to observe that the import prices for oranges almost always peak in July or August. The price change exceeds 100% and happens every year. The same magnitude or nature of variation is not seen in banana imports. This allows us to understand the relatively higher price variation of oranges compared to bananas that we established previously.

Summary

With two datasets, we were able to compare the prices of food commodities. We then dived deep into a comparison of the imported prices of oranges and bananas in United States. We made use of five chart types that helped to give us a better understanding of how bananas correlate with respect to oranges, although we did not attempt to quantify the relationship between banana and orange import prices. Still, we were able to understand how they differed in a very significant way.

In the next chapter, we will visualize relationships as graphs instead of coordinates on orthogonal axes. This will help us to visualize features in a dataset connected in a network.

6
Drawing Connections between Entity Columns

Correlation is a statistical function to measure how two features are related. When feature columns have discrete values, we can measure co-occurrence by plotting joint distributions. But co-occurrence is sometimes insufficient for discovering the semantics of a relationship.

The concept of co-occurrence can be generalized if we think of it as one type of interaction. Many such types of interactions can be defined between discrete entities. Multiple interaction variables give us a better shot at being more effective when encapsulating some form of relatedness.

Interactions can be directed or undirected. Datasets containing entities can be visualized as directed (or undirected) flow graphs. The edges between entities are the interaction variables that we can analyze. Our goal in this chapter is to make charts that help us to visualize and analyze datasets that contain entity identifiers and directed (or undirected) relationship values defining pair-wise relationships between entities.

We will create charts to visualize entities and relationships—as networks with nodes, edges, and via flow graphs. In this chapter, we will specifically cover:

- Datasets
- Directed force networks
- Chord diagrams
- Sunburst chart
- Sankey's diagram
- Partitioning

Datasets

Data on bilateral trade flowing between nations fits right into the definition of a dataset with entities and relationships to explore. Katherine Barbieri, University of South Carolina, and Omar Keshk, Ohio State University, maintain a dataset that tracks the flow of trade between nations between 1870 and 2017. Amounts are converted to their equivalent US dollar values as of 2014.

The dataset is available publicly as part of *The Correlates of War Project*. Here is the link to the project: `http://www.correlatesofwar.org/data-sets/bilateral-trade`. We will be using version 4.0 of this dataset in this chapter.

The IMF's **Direction of Trade Statistics** (**DOTS**) quarterly release shares trade data between nations and is a source from which the project aggregates data. It is important to specify that DOTS includes only the trade value of merchandise (or ready-to-sell goods) , as mentioned at this link: `http://datahelp.imf.org/knowledgebase/articles/484354-why-is-the-trade-data-in-the-direction-of-trade-st`.

Because the schema of the tabular dataset on the website is not in the form of `timestamp`, `entity_A`, `entity_B`, `relationship_value_B`, and other feature columns, I have created a Python script to transform the dataset before loading it into our Superset web app. First, clone the book's GitHub repository from this link: `https://github.com/PacktPublishing/Superset-Quick-Start-Guide`. Then, just go to `Chapter06` and download file `COW_Trade_4.0` and `Dyadic_COW_4.0_modified.csv`. You will also find the Python script and the original dataset from *The Correlates of War Project* website in the same directory for reference. Use the **Upload a CSV** feature to load the file.

Besides four column values of **importer**, **exporter**, **trade flow**, and **year**, the prepared dataset carries two features from the original, spike and dip. The definition of these columns, as given in the corresponding dataset document, is: *a spike was considered to have occurred and labeled as 1, if the percentage change in flow at time t was greater than 50% and, simultaneously, the percentage change in flow at time t+1 was less than 50%.*

A dip in trade values was considered to have occurred and was labeled as one, if the percentage change in flow at time t was less than 50% and, simultaneously, the percentage change in flow at time *t+1* was greater than 50%. Before we move on to making charts, after uploading the `COW_Trade_4.0` and `Dyadic_COW_4.0_modified.csv` files, make sure you update the **Column** attributes such that they reflect their use:

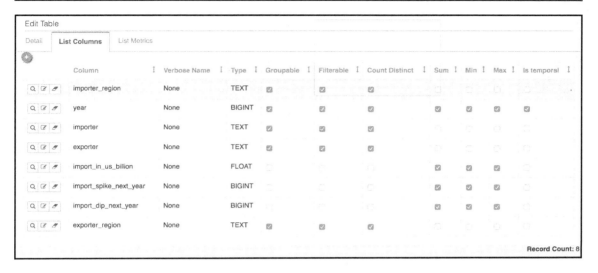

List Columns displaying the columns attributes

Directed force networks

By using a directed force network, we can analyze the value of the imports nations exchange with each other. The time granularity of this dataset is in years. The time filter box available in Superset is easy to interpret and use for time columns that are more granular than yearly. Just select the **clear** option on it; we will not use it:

The time filter box

In the **Query** box, select the **exporter** column as the **Source** and **importer** column as the **Target**. The **Metric** function we choose will be irrelevant. Because this is time series data we are dealing with, we will inspect the trade flow between the nation entities for a specific year only. Therefore, there will be only one record for each **exporter**, **importer** directed relationship. You can use **AVG** or any other **Metric** function; the result will be the same:

Setting parameters for trade imports that spiked after 2009

In the **Filters** section, limit it to records that have **2010** in their **year** column. This will provide a 2010 time snapshot of the trade flow between nations. Given the large number of nations that trade, we can make our analysis richer and more fruitful by focusing on specific types of trade flow – the ones that boomed after 2009. To do this, add another filter, where only records that have the value **1** for **import_spike_next_year** are selected.

This is how it will look:

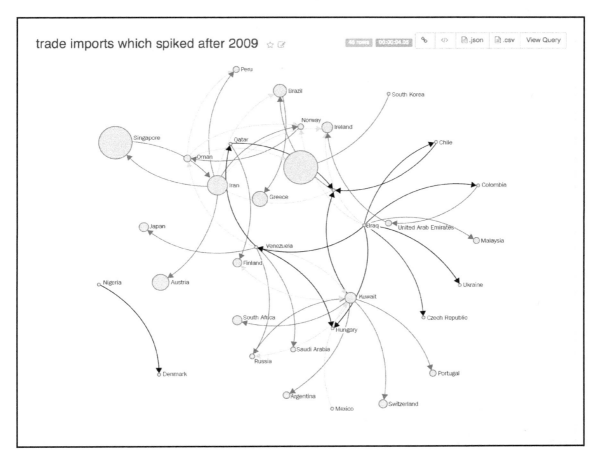

The trade imports which spiked after 2009

Aha! We have a beautiful directed network showing the volume of imports for the trade relationships that spiked by at least 50% after 2009. The size of each node is its total import value. Sweden and Singapore stand out as two nations that imported a lot more, relative to other nations that also increased their imports after 2009.

Now, let's invert the question we are asking this dataset and filter 2010 records or trade relationships that dipped after 2009, in 2010. You have to update the second filter in the **Filters** section, by changing it from **import_spiked_next_year** to **import_dip_next_year**:

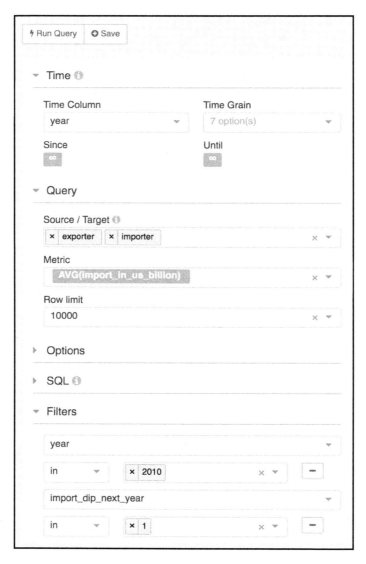

Setting parameters for trade imports that dipped after 2009

Notice that the UAE, which had a spike in imports from Columbia that was greater than 50%, reduced its imports from Slovakia by more than 50%. However, the big importer in this snapshot—the United Kingdom—did not have import spikes with any nation in the year 2010. Switzerland, on the other hand, reduced its imports from South Africa but increased its imports from Kuwait.

This is how this will look:

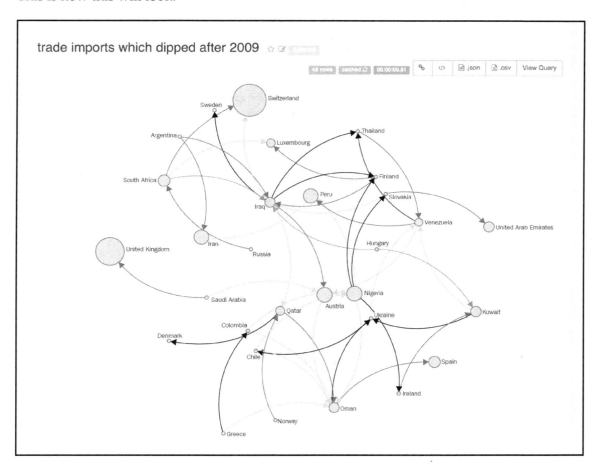

The trade imports which dipped after 2009

This visualization has a lot to tell us about nations who have traded with each other over time. With contextual knowledge about global trade, economics, and geopolitical relations, we could describe and visualize this dataset better. However, that would be out of the scope of this book, so let's make another chart!

Chord diagrams

Using a directed network diagram, we were able to identify the nations that experienced a spike or dip in their imports from other nations in 2010. We also noticed the nations that imported the most in that visualization. How about we now ask the question: which country exported more than they imported in 2014? How much did they import or export? Let's say we already have a list of nations in which we are interested, and they happen to be China, Germany, India, Japan, the United Kingdom, and the United States.

We will use a chord diagram to do this. The filter conditions on the year 2014 and the list of trading nations in which we are interested can be specified in the **Custom WHERE clause** text field:

```
(exporter="United Kingdom" OR exporter="Japan" OR exporter="China" OR
exporter="Germany" OR exporter="India" OR exporter="United States of
America")
AND (importer="United Kingdom" OR importer="China" OR importer="Germany" OR
importer="India" OR importer="United States of America" OR
importer="Japan")
AND year=2014
```

In the **Source** field, set **exporter** and in the **Target** field, set **importer** as input into the columns. You can set **SUM(import_in_us_billion)** in the **Metric** column:

⚡ Run Query   ⊕ Save

Data   Style

▾ Datasource & Chart Type

Datasource
`Dyadic_COW_4.0_modified` ✐ ⊕

Visualization Type
`Chord Diagram`

▾ Time ⓘ

Time Column	Time Grain
year ▾	7 option(s) ▾

Since	Until
∞	∞

▾ Query

Source	Target
exporter × ▾	importer × ▾

Metric	Row limit
`SUM(import_in_us_billion)` × ▾	10000 × ▾

▾ SQL ⓘ

Custom WHERE clause
```
1   (exporter="United Kingdom" OR exporter="Japan" OR exporter="China" OR exp
2   AND (importer="United Kingdom" OR importer="China" OR importer="Germany"
3   AND year=2014
```

Custom HAVING clause
```
1
```

▾ Filters

＋ Add Filter

Setting parameters for the chord diagram to display imports of countries in 2014

The output will be as follows:

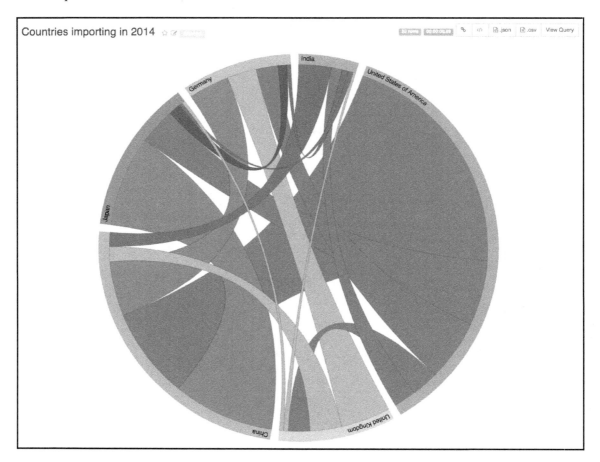

Chord diagram displaying imports of countries in 2014

The chord connecting two arcs, representing two nations in the circle, has a dominating arc color based on the nation that exports more. We can see that the United States dominates all five trade relationships. Only India and the United States exported more to China than China exported to them. We can also see the metric values in the chord diagram, when hovering over a chord:

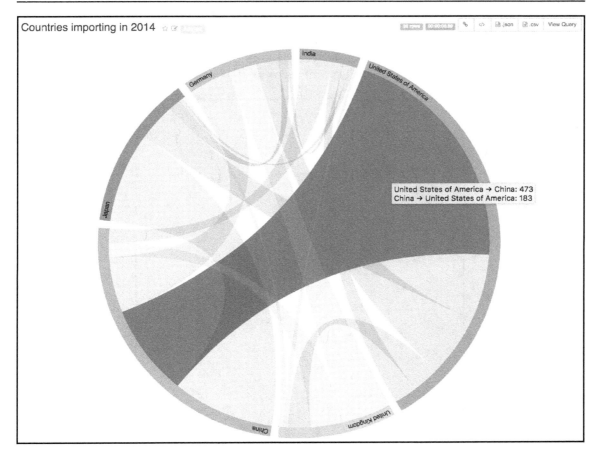

Viewing metric values by hovering over the chord

The metric value here means that the United States exported 473 billion USD worth of goods to China, while China exported 183 billion USD to the United States in 2014.

That was a fun fact! Let's move on to making more charts.

Sunburst chart

Sometimes, it is useful to measure relationships between entities relative to a common denominator. In the case of trade flow data, let's try to visualize the fraction of the global export that each nation services. To do this, we will use a Sunburst chart.

We will take a snapshot of the time-series data and select the trade flow that took place in the year 2013. For this, we will use the **Custom Where clause**. In the **Hierarchy** field, set **exporter** and **importer** as the parent-child relationship. In the **Primary Metric**, select **SUM(import_in_us_billion)** and set its name as **total_trade_volume**:

Setting parameters for the Sunburst diagram to display trade flow in 2013

Perfect! Now just click on **Run Query** to render your Sunburst chart **Global Trade Flow Between Nations in 2013**:

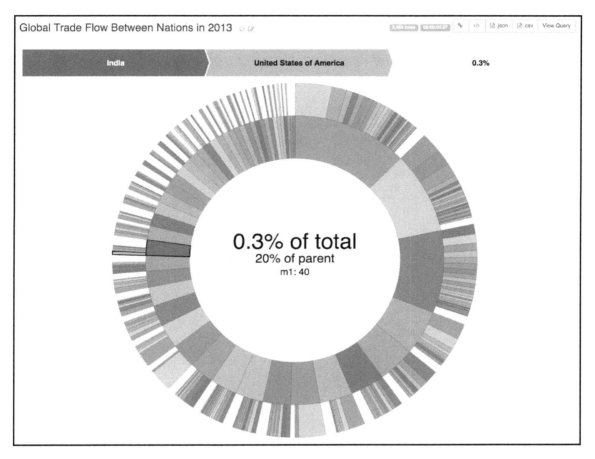

The Sunburst diagram displaying trade flow in 2013

Selecting a parent entity from the inner circle and a child entity from the outer circle displays the fraction of global trade the relationship represents. It also shows the metric value, which is the total trade volume exported by India to the US in 2013 – 40 billion USD. This value represents 0.3% of the global trade volume. This trade volume, as previously stated, is based on IMF's DOTS, which only accounts for merchandise goods. There are other commodities and services that nations trade, such as financial services, which are not accounted for. The 40 billion USD value represents 20% of the trade volume that India exported in the year 2013.

You can have fun with the visualization by selecting different pairs of nations, such as China and the United States, to see what fraction of Chinese exports are imported by the United States and compare it to the fraction of the United States' exports that China imports to understand trade relations between nations.

Sankey's diagram

Sankey diagrams are flow diagrams where the width of the arrows is shown as proportional to the flow quantity. We will use one to understand from where merchandise goods imported into Western European nations originate. Because the number of nations that export to Western European nations is too large to visualize, we will group trade flow by the geographical regions of the exporting nations:

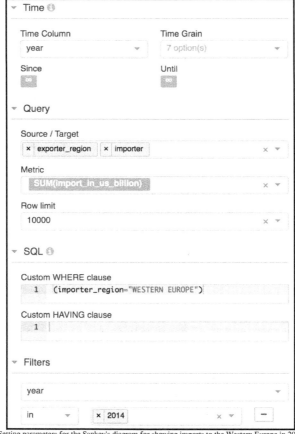

Setting parameters for the Sankey's diagram for showing imports to the Western Europe in 2014

The **Since** and **Until** fields in the **Time** section can be cleared because we will use **2014** as the value in the **year** column to filter rows in the dataset. Groups of nations can be represented using the value in their **exporter_region** as the **Source** field and **importer** column to represent the Western European nations. In order to only select a Western European country as the **Target** or the importing nation in the flow diagram, we insert some custom SQL code in the **Custom WHERE clause**:

```
(importer_region="WESTERN EUROPE")
```

Now, just the select **Sankey** as the chart type and generate a chart showing the trade flow between geographical regions and Western European countries in the year 2014.

This is how it will look:

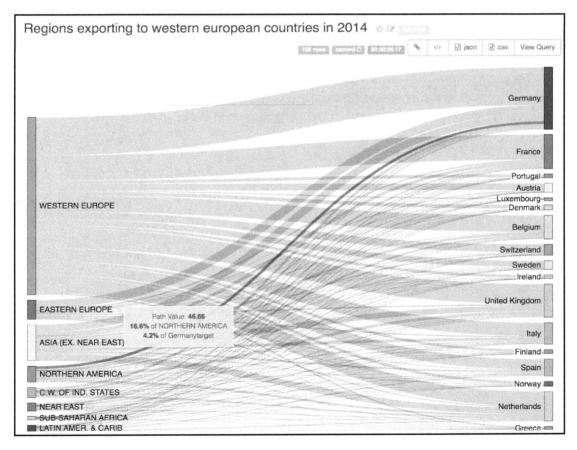

Sankey's graph showing imports to the western Europe in 2014

Each flow arrow also has a tooltip listing the flow quantity, which, in our case, is 46.66 billion USD worth of goods exported from Northern America to Germany. This value represents 16.6% of the total value traded with Western European nations. Germany imports significantly more from other Western European nations closer to it, Eastern European nations, and Asia (excluding the Near East/Middle East) compared to Northern America.

Partitioning

We can visualize how much nations in a particular geographical region import from other regions in a different way, using partition diagrams called **TreeMaps**. We will create a filter to select records for Asian (excluding Near East) nations. The first partitions will be proportional to the total import trade volume of each Asian nation. Then, each nation's partition will be further partitioned to show how much and in what proportions the nation imports from different geographical regions.

The nations controlling the largest area in the first partition will be the nations dominating the import market in Asia (excluding the Near East). The larger partitions inside each nation will represent the export market that supplies most of the merchandise goods to the corresponding Asian nation:

Setting parameters for the partition graph to display Asian nations imports in 2014

We will configure the chart with the same values as the Sankey diagram and update the SQL code in the **Custom WHERE clause** field:

```
(importer_region="WESTERN EUROPE")
```

Now, let's generate the TreeMap!

This is how it will look:

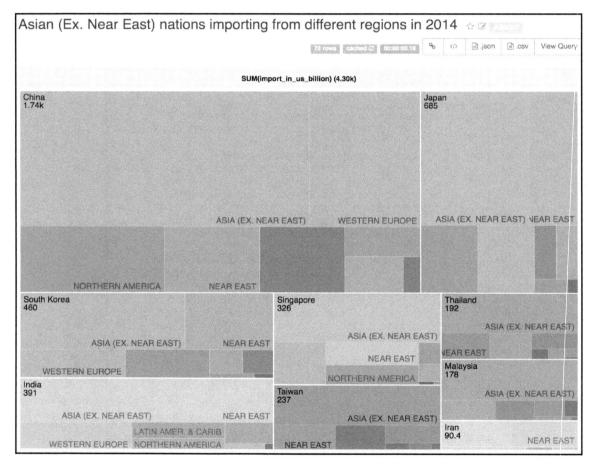

The partition graph displaying Asian nations imports in 2014

Here, we can see that the top four importing nations in 2014 – China, Japan, South Korea, and India – imported more from each other than any other geographical region. After Asian nations, China imported the most from Western Europe, while the other three imported the most from Near-East nations.

This chart is interactive. We can select one of the nations that does not have a big import market to look into its distribution, which will be dwarfed by the big four. Let's click on **Malaysia**:

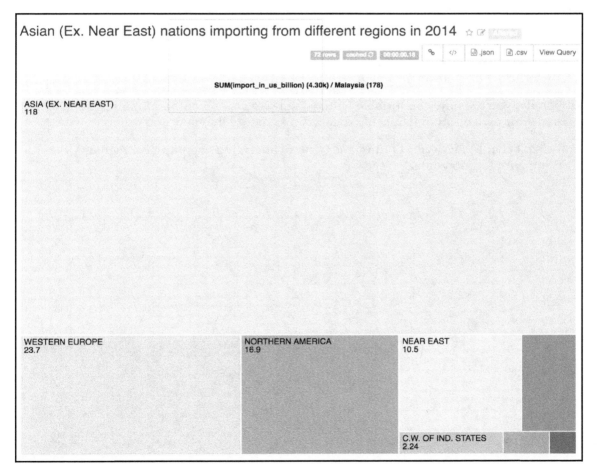

Selecting a particular country(Malaysia) to get in-depth information of the imports

This feature allows us to read the values using proportionally scaled areas for each entity according to the amount of imports it represents. In the case of Malaysia, we can see that it imported 2.24 billion USD worth of goods in 2014 from the Commonwealth of Individual States, where the major exporters are Russia and Ukraine.

Summary

We made a lot of charts in this chapter! Those were just some approaches to visualizing and analyzing a dataset with entities and a value quantifying a type of relationship. The Superset chart, called a partition diagram, is similar to a TreeMap, but it only generates a single level of partitioning. So, I chose to use a TreeMap instead of that, because it provided a more efficient and powerful way to visualize data.

Hopefully, you are now comfortable with using these chart examples for inspiration to upload your own entity-relationship dataset and analyze it in new and different ways.

In the next chapter, we will continue the trend of analyzing geographical regions by working with location data.

7
Mapping Data That Has Location Information

Location information in datasets represents something we can relate to. It is about points existing in our world. This makes it one of the most interesting types of dataset for analysis. But it is not intuitive to view location coordinates without geographical maps. This makes the task of data analysis and the summarizing of location coordinates without a geographical map a bit of a challenge. However, services such as **Mapbox** and **deck.gl** provide a variety of apps and APIs for visualizing location information on beautiful maps.

In this chapter, we will render location data as scatter plots on maps as follows:

- A scatter point
- A scatter grid

Then, we will plot arcs and lines on a map:

- Arcs
- Path

Remember, the MAPBOX_API_KEY variable in the superset_config.py file that we wrote in the Superset configuration chapter? That API key must be initialized before proceeding with this chapter, since Superset will map tiles for charts using Mapbox APIs.

Data

In this chapter, we will make use of two datasets. First, we will download the global list of airports as of 2017. We will download it from the OpenFlights website. They have multiple datasets—airports, airlines, routes, and aeroplanes in use. These are available on their data page at: https://openflights.org/data.html.

This is how it should appear: https://github.com/PacktPublishing/Superset-Quick-Start-Guide/blob/master/Graphics/Chapter%207/Chart%201.png

We will fetch the airports dataset from the following GitHub link: https://raw.githubusercontent.com/jpatokal/openflights/master/data/airports.dat. Some changes have to be made before uploading it. In the Chapter07 directory for the GitHub repository, you will find the generate_dataset.ipynb Jupyter Notebook. Run it to create the two datasets.

This is the code for creating the airports_modified.csv file:

```
import pandas as pd
!wget
https://raw.githubusercontent.com/jpatokal/openflights/master/data/airports
.dat
columns = [
    "Airport ID",
    "Name",
    "City",
    "Country",
    "IATA",
    "ICAO",
    "Latitude",
    "Longitude",
    "Altitude",
    "Timezone",
    "DST",
    "Tz",
    "Type",
    "Source"
]
df = pd.read_csv('airports.dat', delimiter=',', doublequote=True,
header=-1, names=columns)
df.to_csv('airports_modified.csv', index=False)
!rm airports.dat
```

After loading the CSV, make sure the **Column** attributes of the table have suitable values:

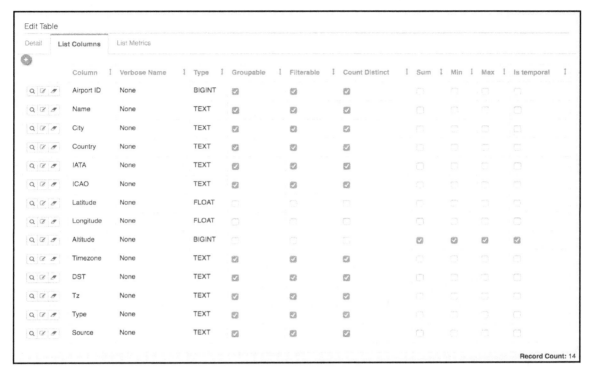

Values of the Column attributes in the CSV file

The second dataset contains California's rail routes. The California Department of Fish and Wildlife has a shape file highlighting rail routes in California on which crude oil is transported. The dataset is listed on its web page at `https://map.dfg.ca.gov/metadata/ds1337.html`. The dataset is of the Union Pacific and BNSF routes—the two transporters of crude by rail in California. The `dataset.ipynb` Jupyter Notebook has the Python code to modify the dataset before uploading it. The original dataset can be found here: `ftp://ftp.dfg.ca.gov/BDB/GIS/BIOS/Public_Datasets/1300_1399/ds1337.zip`

The `Chapter07` directory on GitHub has the output files ready for upload in case you don't want to run the Notebook.

Scatter point

After uploading the `airports_modified.csv` file from the GitHub directory, open the table and select the **Deck.gl - Scatter plot** chart. In the **Query** section, select **Longitude | Latitude** as the coordinates. This dataset contains the locations of all airports across the globe. We will be plotting a point for each airport on the world map.

In the **Point Size** section, set **1000** as the **Point Size** so that each airport location is visible. Using **Dark** as the **Map Style** and discernible colors for showing country-wise color scheme, we will make the chart easy to understand:

Setting the parameters for plotting a point to each airport on the world map

This is how the scatter points will appear: `https://github.com/PacktPublishing/Superset-Quick-Start-Guide/blob/master/Graphics/Chapter%207/Chart%202.png`

In 2017, we can see a world with regions that have significantly different densities of airports. Such map data may be overlaid with population density data to interpret the densities with respect to another map feature, and together they will make more sense.

Scatter grid

We will use the same **airports_2017** table to see where South-East Asia's largest airports are located:

Using the Filters option to select airports in South-East Asian countries

After you select **Visualization Type**, use the **Filters** option present in the **Query** section for selecting airports in South-East Asian countries as follows:

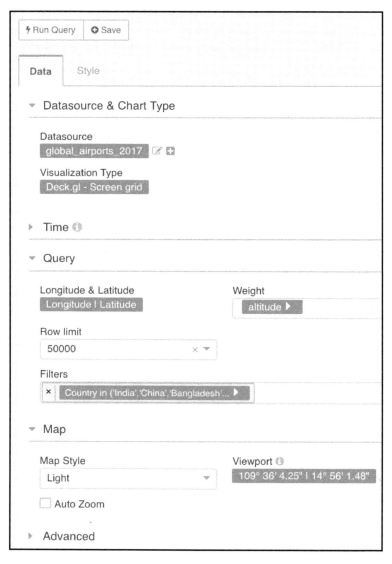

Setting the parameters for plotting South-East Asia's largest airports

You can change the **Viewport** of the **Map** to view it at an angle. Grid boxes representing airports in the Sichuan and Gansu provinces in China, and Jammu and Kashmir in India, have the densest color, implying they are at higher altitudes compared to other regions with airports.

This is how it will appear:

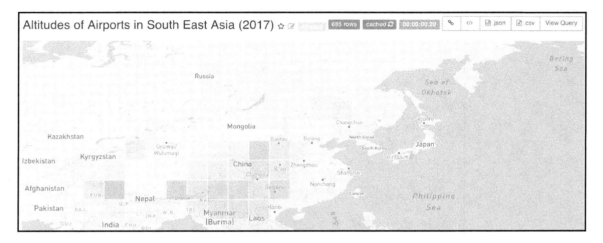

Overview of South-East Asia's largest airports (the other place names are not important)

Arcs

After taking a close look at airports in South-East Asia, let's take a view of global flight routes. We saw that there are many airports almost everywhere on the world map. There will be exponentially more flight routes. So, to get a view of flight routes that we can comprehend and summarize while looking at one chart, we filter for flight routes that start from the city of Tehran, in Iran:

Setting the parameters for flight routes across Asia

You can select **Fixed Color** and **Stroke Width** to change the aesthetics of the **Arc** map. We can see that Iran in 2017 has only one international flight route, to Saudi Arabia:

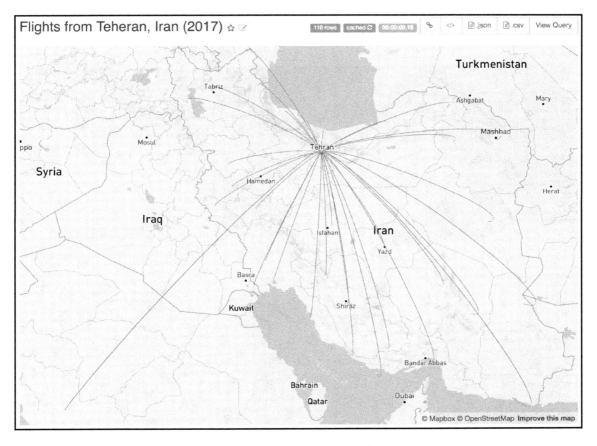

The flight routes in Asia (the other place names are not important)

We will now use the **Map Style** feature of the **Arc** chart to use satellite images. This time, we select one of the largest cities in the world, and one that is mentioned in the chronicles—Dhaka. For this chart, the **Map Style** is **Satellite**:

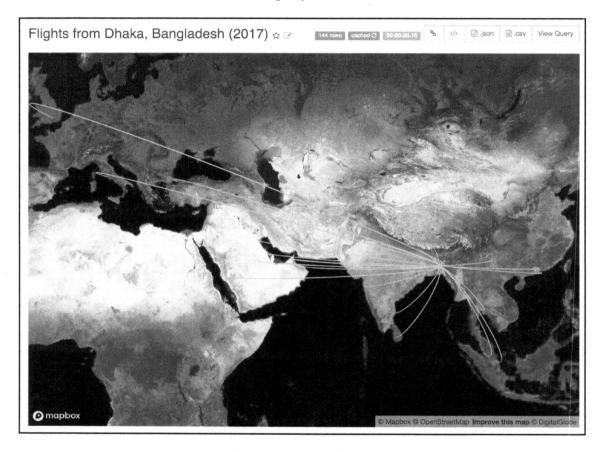

An overview of the Map Style for displaying the flight routes

You can notice that in 2017, Dhaka had flights to its South-East Asian neighbors and a few to the Middle East, along with flights to three other countries in Europe—the United Kingdom, Turkey, and Italy.

Path

Routes are often found in location datasets to represent road or rail networks. We can plot those types of datasets using the **Path** visualization option. After uploading the rail routes dataset, either by downloading from the GitHub directory or creating it using the Jupyter Notebook, open it for visualization purposes:

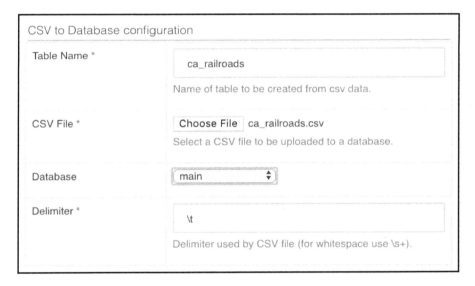

CSV to Database configuration

If you take a look at the Jupyter Notebook, you will find that we create a feature named **Polyline**. It uses geometry information given in the file. Polylines are an encoded representation of latitudes and longitudes, as follows:

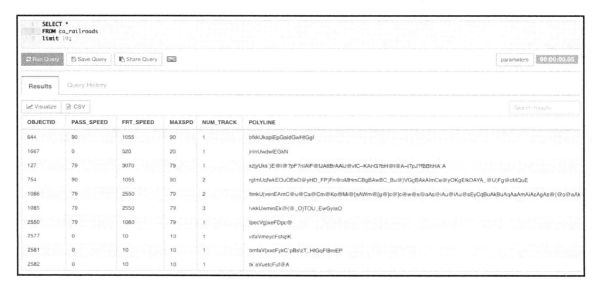

Encoded representation of latitudes and longitudes

The dataset represents rail routes over which crude oil is transported. It might be helpful to locate it on map tiles made of satellite imagery, because we can then see terrain information pertaining to the rail routes.

The bearing value in the **Viewport** option helps us to drive the viewer's focus along the most interesting angle toward the map. The pitch defines the z axis value to the bearing axes. The right pitch value enables the viewer to quickly identify elevation level differences on a map:

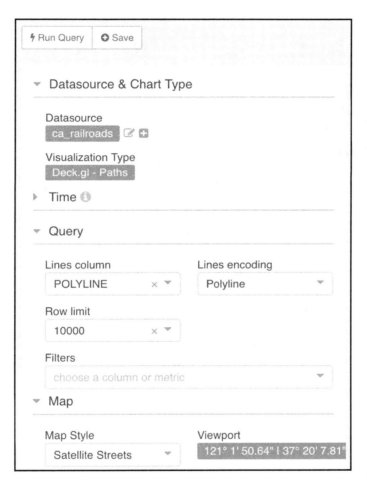

Setting the parameters for the rail routes

This dataset was published in 2014. We can see that rail routes are dense around the Los Angeles and San Francisco city districts:

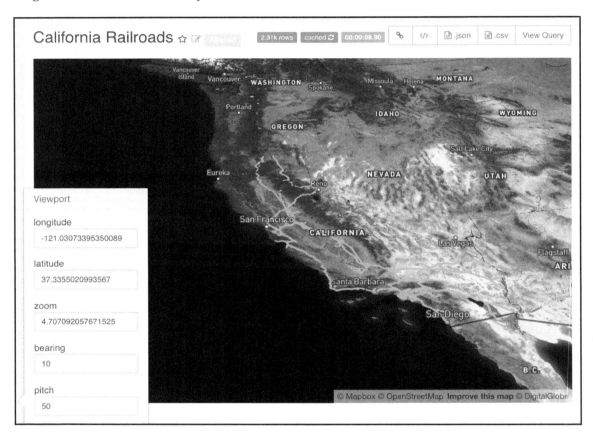

An overview of California rail routes (the other place names are not important)

Summary

In this chapter, we made charts using latitudes, longitudes, and attributes such as altitude features. It helped us to visualize two flight networks, and routes on geographical maps. With technologies such as GPS and satellite imagery, more location data is being generated. We now know how to visualize and analyze such datasets on Superset.

In the next chapter, we will make some beautiful dashboards and complete our Superset quick-start journey.

8
Building Dashboards

Dashboards are reporting tools for visually analyzing key data points and tracking insightful metrics. Effective dashboards have layouts that distribute screen space proportionally, based on the reader's required attention for each chart. The chart type and its position on a dashboard affect the readability of data points and their meaning in the overarching story flow of the dashboard.

We have made many types of charts in our book, and our goal was to answer a set of related questions for each dataset. In this chapter, we'll try to organize the charts so that the dashboard is effective at coherently communicating those answers. We'll cover the following topics:

- Charts
- Dashboards

Charts

Let's take a look at the charts made in this book. Then, we'll analyze example dashboards made using those charts.

Getting started with Superset

We looked at the dataset of Stack Overflow questions between 2008 and part of 2018. We visualized the number of questions per year and noted accelerated growth between 2008-2013 and slower growth afterward, using a line chart:

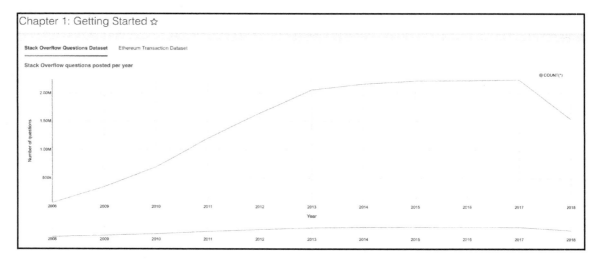

Overview of the Stack Overflow questions dataset

We plotted the Ethereum transaction volume and noted the increase between 2015 and 2018:

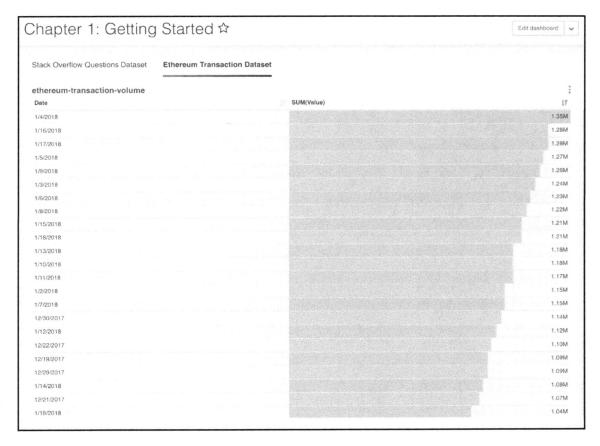

Overview of the Ethereum transaction dataset

Visualizing data in a column

In this chapter, we picked the reading log from `http://austinrochford.com/` for data analysis.

With five charts, we were able to get insights about the page count feature in the time series dataset. The histogram and bar chart provided information about the page count and number of reading days for the books in the dataset. Such charts, when put on a dashboard, provide useful context before analysis:

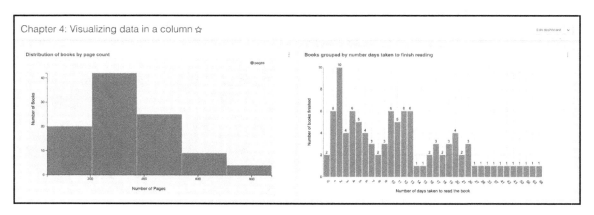

Chart for distribution of books by page count

Box plots and dual axis line charts showed the variance in page count values for different groups of books defined by the number of reading days:

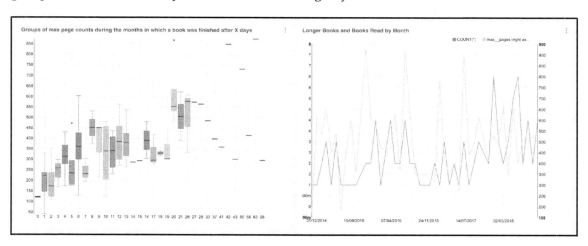

Box plots and dual axis line charts showing the variance in page count values

Finally, a headline chart was used to summarize the dataset by displaying the page count read per day on average, across all books:

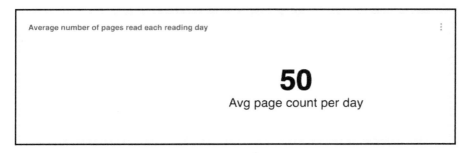

Headline chart to summarize the dataset

Comparing feature values

With the Federal Bank of St. Louis and **United States Department of Agriculture (USDA)** food commodities dataset, we investigated trends in the seasonal price of commodities such as oranges and bananas:

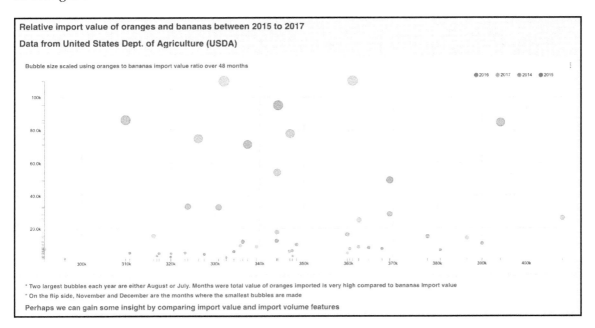

Bubble chart displaying import values of the commodities

First, we identified the two commodities with similar price values over time. After that, we diveded the import data into oranges and bananas. Finally, using four additional charts, we learned about a plausible connection between the harvesting times of fruits and import prices:

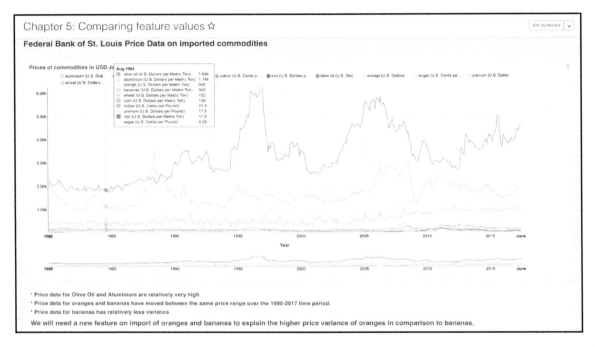

Chart displaying feature values on imported commodities

The following graph shows the relative differences between import values and volumes for the commodities (oranges and bananas):

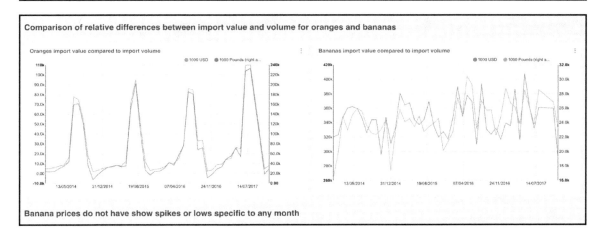

Comparison of relative differences for bananas and oranges

The following graph shows the seasonal spikes of oranges during July and August:

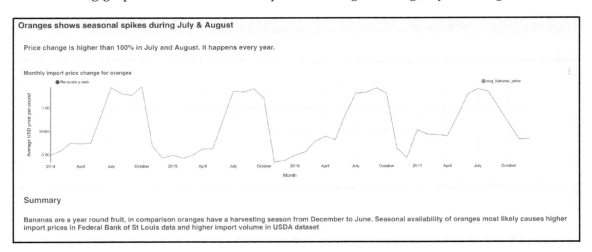

Chart showing the seasonal spikes of oranges during July and August

Drawing connections between entity columns

The trade flow numbers between nations present in the IMF's **Direction of Trade Statistics (DOTS)** quarterly release dataset were visualized using multiple charts.

Each chart showed differences in trade volumes in USD between nations as entities. Using a Sankeys graph, a sunburst, a chord diagram, and a directed force graph, we looked at different groups of nations and their relative differences in trade volume. TreeMap was effective at showing the breakdown of import volumes in USD for countries, grouped by region:

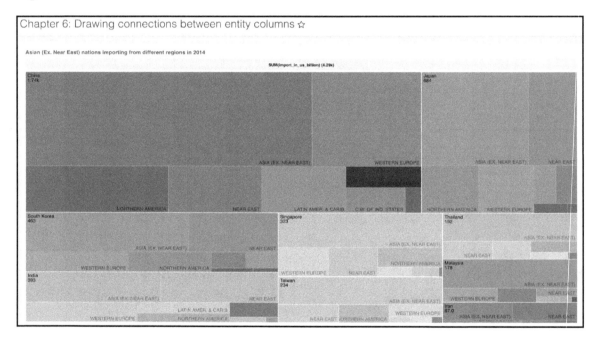

An overview of the partition chart drawing connections between entity columns (the other names are not important)

Mapping data that has location information

We used two datasets in Chapter 7, *Mapping Data That Has Location Information*, to visualize geographic coordinates for airports, flight routes, and a subset of railroads in California, United States. You can view it in the following link:

```
https://github.com/PacktPublishing/Superset-Quick-Start-Guide/blob/master/
Graphics/Chapter%208/Chart%201.png
```

In the first dataset, we identified altitudes at which different airports are built across the world. We also saw the flight connections between Iran and rest of the world, followed by a similar chart for Bangladesh.

Then, using the second dataset, we zoomed into a `deck.gl` map that showed how railroad tracks that transport crude oil connect different cities and towns in California.

We didn't make any charts for `Chapter 2`, *Configuring Superset and Using SQL Lab*, or `Chapter 3`, *User Authentication and Permissions*, because they were all about configuring, deploying, and managing permissions for Superset.

Dashboards

A dashboard layout presents a set of charts in a way that viewers can scan them and get key insight. Layouts make use of different components such as a heading, divider, and data filters.

We'll work with all of the dashboard components available in the Superset v0.28 release. By breaking down examples, we'll create the dashboards for `Chapter 1`, *Getting Started with Data Exploration*; `Chapter 5`, *Comparing Feature Values*; and `Chapter 7`, *Mapping Data That Has Location Information*. Our familiarity with the charts and the dataset will be critical in helping us to make the right decisions about the layout.

Hopefully, in this section, we'll improve our intuition for building dashboard layouts that are effective in reporting insights for any set of charts.

Making a dashboard

On the dashboards page, select **Add a new record** to create a new dashboard instance, as follows:

Creating a dashboard instance

This will open the configuration page for the dashboard. Here, we can insert the dashboard **Title** text and a readable string to use in the dashboard URL:

Configuration page of the dashboard

Once you **Save** the form, the dashboard is ready to get some charts.

Selecting charts

In the edit mode, use the **Select charts and filters** option to search for the charts that you want to add. For the **Chapter 1: Getting Started** dashboard, we'll add **Stack Overflow questions posted per year**:

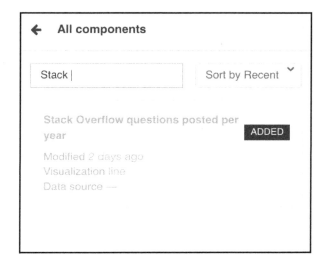

Search option for adding charts

This is then followed by **Ethereum Transaction Volume** as the second chart. The charts do not represent insights from the same dataset. It's important therefore that we separate them into two tabs.

Separating charts into tabs

We have added two charts to our first dashboard. Next, we'll insert a component with which we can place charts on different tabs:

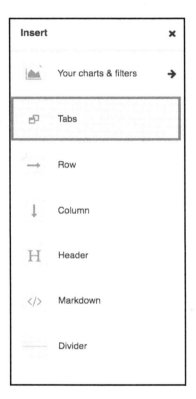

The Tabs option

After you insert the **Tabs** component, just drag and drop the two charts. Once the two charts have been separated, label the tabs with the corresponding dataset names represented in the charts:

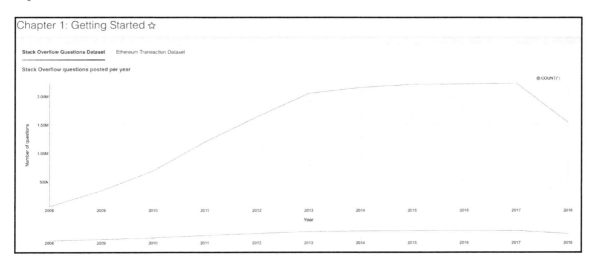

Chart showing the Stack Overflow questions dataset

Headlining sections using titles

In Chapter 5, *Comparing Feature Values*, we used multiple datasets: one from the Federal Bank of St. Louis, containing the prices of globally traded commodities over the years 1980-2017, and the second from the USDA, containing import volumes and values of oranges and bananas.

The insight from the data analysis makes use of both datasets. The analysis progresses like a simple story. We can make use of **Header** component to properly introduce the story flow to the dashboard viewer. You will find it in the list of components, as follows:

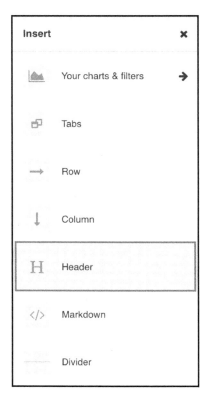

The Header option

The **Header** component is useful to clearly introduce important charts on the dashboard.

You can find it here:

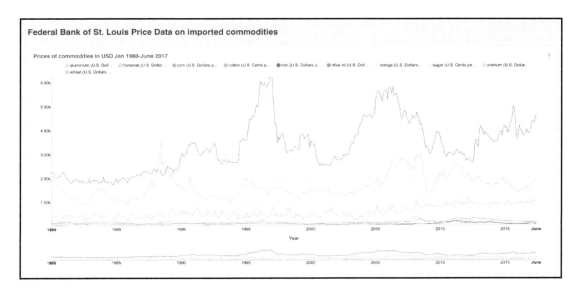

Chart showing the imported commodities of the Federal Bank of St. Louis

Multiple headlines can be used to introduce a new dataset along with a new chart:

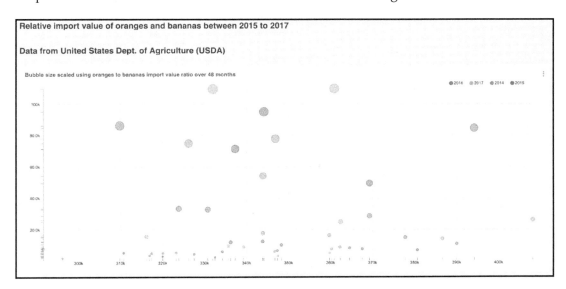

Bubble chart showing the relative import values of oranges and bananas between 2015-2017

Inserting markdown

The **Markdown** component on a dashboard provides space for describing insights from the chart or related information that the viewer might find useful in connecting the story on the dashboard:

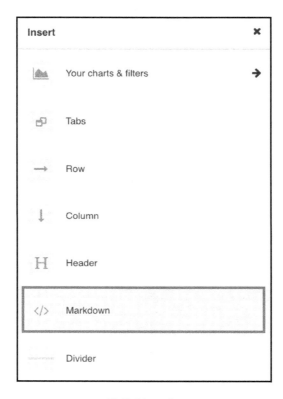

The Markdown option

In the data analysis in `Chapter 5`, *Comparing Feature Values,* we started with a hypothesis that seasonality of orange harvests and year-around banana harvests might be related to the much higher variance in orange import prices.

Key insights about the price change for the two commodities, bananas and oranges, can be captured in the **Markdown** components. After a clear presentation of the data showing that the orange harvesting season between December and June is in sync with lower price change periods, the validated hypothesis was presented in the end with special markdown font formatting:

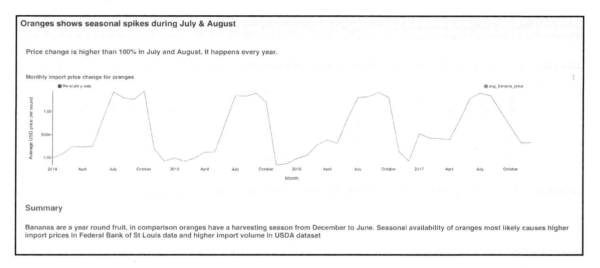

Chart showing the seasonal spikes of oranges during July and August

After a clear presentation of charts showing that the orange harvesting season between December and June also sees low price changes in those months. The validated hypothesis is presented in the end with special markdown font formatting, so that our final finding is reported effectively to the dashboard viewer.

Organizing charts in the dashboard layout

In Chapter 7, *Mapping Data That Has Location Information,* we analyzed two datasets. The first dataset had information about airports around the world. We used it to visualize how the airports are distributed across countries and continents. Since we had altitude as a feature, we used the screen grid chart type to distinguish airports in South East Asia on a map with its altitude color-coded. Finally, we looked at flight routes from Dhaka, Bangladesh and Teheran, Iran to places around the world.

The first chart requires much more screen space, because it shows points on a much larger geographical area, although less so in the case of South East Asian airports. To achieve this, we can resize the first chart to take up a wider horizontal area in comparison to other charts.

We'll make use of **Column** components to vertically align the South East Asian airports altitude chart to the first one and subtract column space from its left and right:

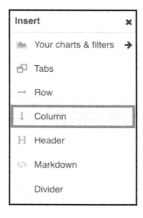

The Column option

In order to present a contrast between flight routes from Dhaka and Teheran, we can use the **Column** components. Instead of creating two empty column, in the case of the previous chart, we can create two equally sized **Column** components and fill them with the two charts.

The first chart can be found as follows:

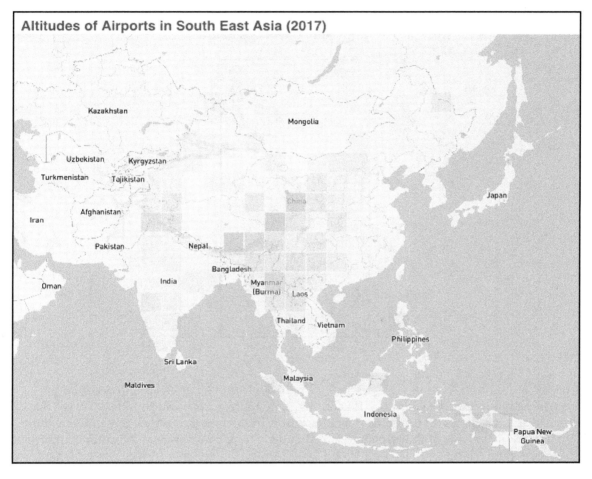

An overview of altitudes of the airports in South East Asia (2017) (the other places are not important)

The second chart can be found at this link: `https://github.com/PacktPublishing/Superset-Quick-Start-Guide/blob/master/Graphics/Chapter%208/Chart%202.png`

Separating sections using dividers

The **Divider** component is an effective way to separate sections on a dashboard. We can insert it, just like the **Row** and **Column** components, as follows:

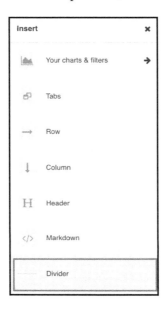

The Divider option

The second dataset in `Chapter 7`, *Mapping Data That Has Location Information*, contains information about railroad routes. It is on the same topic, transportation. Because we want to present both charts on the same dashboard, it is important that we clearly indicate the separation in analysis of the two charts. This can be done by inserting a **Divider** component to separate the charts.

The chart can be found at this link: `https://github.com/PacktPublishing/Superset-Quick-Start-Guide/blob/master/Graphics/Chapter%208/Chart%203.png`

Summary

We have completed building multiple dashboards in Superset, using charts we built in previous chapters. Now, it is time for you to head out to do some data exploration, analysis, and storytelling on your own!

Other Books You May Enjoy

If you enjoyed this book, you may be interested in these other books by Packt:

Hands-On Data Visualization with Bokeh
Kevin Jolly

ISBN: 9781789135404

- Installing Bokeh and understanding its key concepts
- Creating plots using glyphs, the fundamental building blocks of Bokeh
- Creating plots using different data structures like NumPy and Pandas
- Using layouts and widgets to visually enhance your plots and add a layer of interactivity
- Building and hosting applications on the Bokeh server
- Creating advanced plots using spatial data

Applied Data Visualization with R and ggplot2
Dr. Tania Moulik

ISBN: 9781789612158

- Set up the R environment, RStudio, and understand structure of ggplot2
- Distinguish variables and use best practices to visualize them
- Change visualization defaults to reveal more information about data
- Implement the grammar of graphics in ggplot2 such as scales and faceting
- Build complex and aesthetic visualizations with ggplot2 analysis methods
- Logically and systematically explore complex relationships
- Compare variables in a single visual, with advanced plotting methods

Leave a review - let other readers know what you think

Please share your thoughts on this book with others by leaving a review on the site that you bought it from. If you purchased the book from Amazon, please leave us an honest review on this book's Amazon page. This is vital so that other potential readers can see and use your unbiased opinion to make purchasing decisions, we can understand what our customers think about our products, and our authors can see your feedback on the title that they have worked with Packt to create. It will only take a few minutes of your time, but is valuable to other potential customers, our authors, and Packt. Thank you!

Index

H

headline 90, 92, 94
histogram 78, 80, 81
HTTPS certification
  setting up 39

I

Internet Security Research Group (ISRG) 39

L

Let's Encrypt
  reference 39
List Base Permissions 65
List Users tool 65
long-running queries 44

M

Mapbox access token
  reference 44
metadata database 33, 34
multiple time series
  comparing 98, 99, 100

N

NGINX reverse proxy
  setting up 37, 38, 39

O

OAuth Google sign-in
  setting up 58, 60, 62, 64

P

partition 132, 134, 135, 136
path 147, 148, 150
permissions
  listing, on Views/Menus 68
PostgreSQL 9
public role 74
Python Enhancement Proposal (PEP) 36

Q

queries
  caching 42

S

Sankey's graph 130, 131
scatter grid 141, 142, 143
scatter plot 140, 141
sections
  headlining, titles used 163, 165
Secure Socket Layer (SSL) 39
security features
  accessing 58
session data
  securing 41
SQL Lab 47, 49, 50, 53
SQLite, to PostgreSQL
  data, migrating from 35
SSL certification
  setting up 39, 40
Stack Overflow Questions Dataset
  overview 152
sunburst chart 127, 129
Superset
  about 7
  configuring 14, 15
  installing 9
  sharing 10, 11, 13

T

table schema
  configuring 24
table
  adding 17
tabs
  charts, separating into 162
time series
  comparing 101, 102, 104
titles
  used, for headlining sections 163, 165
Treemaps 132
trends differences
  identifying, for feature values 105, 107, 109,
  111, 113, 115

U

User's Statistics tool 75

V

Views/Menus
  about 67
  permissions, listing 68
visualization
  creating 18, 20, 21, 22

customizing 24, 26

W

web server
  about 35
  Gunicorn 36
  setting 32